The Cross Stitch Book

The Cross Stitch Book

Mary Gostelow

VNR VAN NOSTRAND REINHOLD COMPANY
NEW YORK CINCINNATI TORONTO LONDON MELBORNE

ISBN 0–442–22870–8
First published 1982 by B. T. Batsford Ltd
London, England

Printed in Great Britain

Published in the United States in 1982
by Van Nostrand Reinhold Company Inc.
135 West 50th Street
New York, NY 10020, U.S.A.

Photography by Martin Gostelow
Line illustrations, project designs and
styling by Mary Gostelow

16 15 14 13 12 11 10 9 8 7 6 5 4 3 2

Library of Congress Cataloging in Publication Data

Gostelow, Mary.
  The cross stitch book.

  Includes index.
  1. Cross-stitch.   I. Title.
TT778.C76G68 1982   746.44   82–8420
ISBN 0–442–22870–8   AACR2

Contents

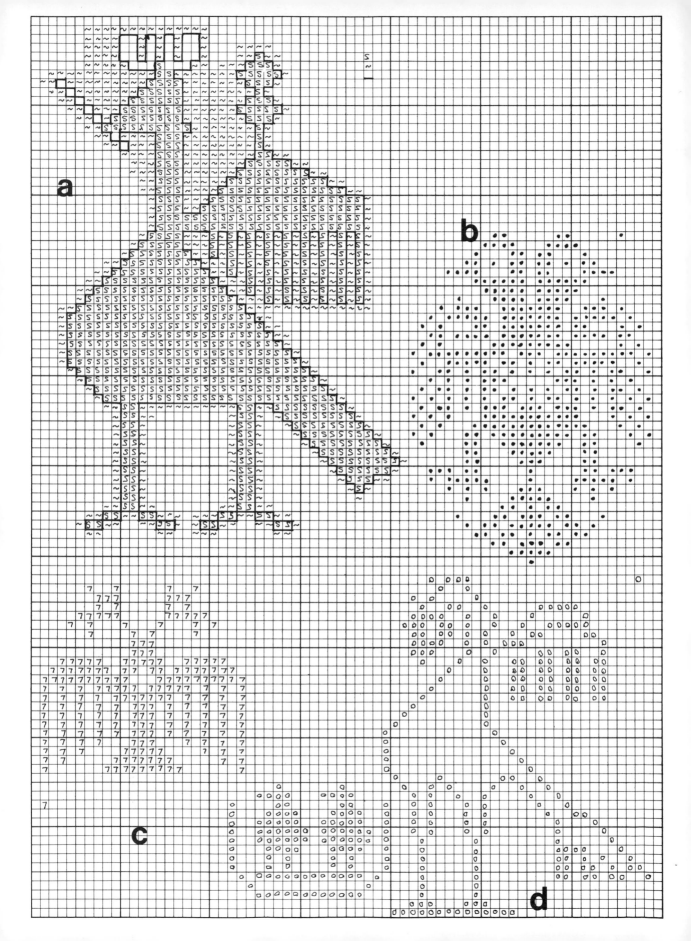

Introduction

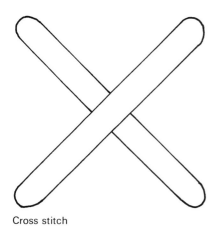

Cross stitch

Left
Birds from (a) Azemmour (b) Spain (c) the Ionian Islands and (d) Hungary.
Azemmour: s   black
             ~   red
                 -outlined in black
                 back stitch
Spain: all black
Ionia and Hungary: red

Cross stitch: probably the oldest decorative stitch in the world and used by every ethnic group in one way or another (Pamela Clabburn, *The Needleworker's Dictionary*, Macmillan and William Morrow, 1976, 172)

The simplest form of cross stitch is *two bisecting diagonals* which form a St Andrew's cross. Generally the two diagonal stitches are at right angles to each other but sometimes the angles are acute or the stitches oblique.

Cross stitch is a *counted thread* technique in that stitches are generally worked over a standard – counted – number of threads of fabric. When people refer to 'counted thread' they often mean cross stitch and only cross stitch, although there are many other embroidery stitches that similarly have to be counted.

There are a myriad variations on, for, from and with cross stitch. This is what my book is all about.

I personally LOVE cross stitch – and I hope you will be equally fascinated with its possibilities.

The book began at lunch one day when my two publishers, Bill Waller and Simon Tuite of Batsford, asked what I wanted to write. In what was I really interested?

"Cross stitch" was my immediate response. Lunch turned into an enthusiastic ideas forum as the concept of the book evolved. My love of history and travel, my interest in people, the fascination of designing, calculating, drawing, stitching and dressmaking and other 'finishing techniques' all came within the scope of this *special embroidery book*.

This is a 'how-to' book at *basic through advanced* levels. If you have never cross stitched before I show you how. If you want revolutionary ideas, I have some to offer.

I did all the drawings, mostly with 0.2, 0.3 and 0.4 Faber-Castell drawing pens.

There are lots of *wearable and usable projects*; you can find them easily by looking up 'Projects' in the index.

Thank you Bill and Simon! And thank you also to Joan Hall in Dorset, Marjorie Littlejohn in Houston and Carol Wesley in Gadsden, Alabama,

for their help with projects. My thanks also to Thelma Nye and Eileen
O'Connor for introducing me to Professor Julius Lessing's 1879 travel
notes and to Louise Kuschak for the introduction to the Bucovina folio.
And my clever friend Iris Clark worked the bouquet on the back cover.

Yes, I knew I was going to enjoy this book – and I hope you do too. I
hope you find it informative, instructional and worthwhile. *Have fun!*

Flowering plants from (a) the
Netherlands and (b) nineteenth century
France.

Netherlands:
s pink
○ green
· yellow
● dark blue
light blue

France:
● dark green
○ light green
s dark pink
7 bright pink

1 Starting cross stitch

Before you start stitching you need to have the proper materials to hand. As you will see, the basic requirements are neither expensive nor demanding.

Basic Cross Stitch Materials:

fabric

needles

threads

scissors

your favourite chair

good light

To follow some of the patterns in this book, and to work on your own designs, you might also like to have ready:

graph paper (I use 20 squares per 5 cm, 10 squares per inch)

notebook and pencils

coloured fibre or felt tip pens or pencils

selection of frames or hoops.

To take the basics first, let me discuss each separately.

Fabric

Cross stitch is traditionally worked on natural or bleached fabric, generally linen. The fabric is sometimes known as 'evenweave', which means that individual warp and weft threads are clearly visible. Stitches are worked in and out of the holes formed between the crossing of the threads.

I work cross stitch more or less exclusively on a linen known as 'Glenshee'. Because it is a natural fibre fabric some warp and weft threads are thicker than others; this gives a 'natural' look to the fabric and to my stitching. Glenshee has approximately 58 threads per 5 cm (29 threads

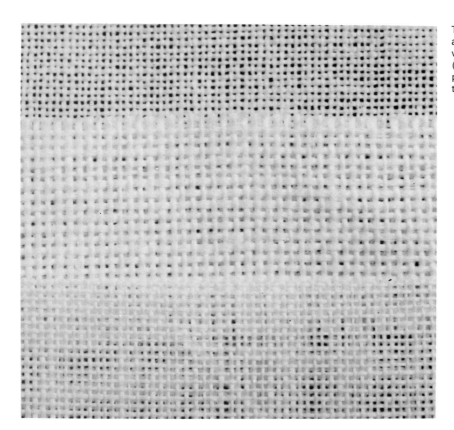

Three of the many different linens available. From top to bottom: Glenshee, with approximately 58 threads per 5 cm (29 per in); Zweigart, with 40 threads per 5 cm (20 per in); Permin, with 50 threads per 5 cm (25 per in)

per inch) which means that if I am cross stitching over two warp and weft threads I have about 29 stitches over every 5 cm (2 in) of fabric.

You may find that one thread of your fabric is particularly heavy or messy. If you want *to disguise a 'messy' thread* there are two things you can do:

1 site your design so that cross stitches will be worked over the 'mess'
2 carefully *pull out* the entire offending thread and weave, in its place, a 'good' thread similarly extracted from surplus of the same fabric.

Linen fabric is *strong*. I am always amazed at the amount of hard handling that a piece on which I am working can take. It also 'softens up' as you work on it.

Linen is *expensive*, though admittedly not as costly as canvas. (Similarly, embroidery threads for cross stitching can cost less than canvaswork or needlepoint threads, and since traditionally not *all* the surface of linen is covered with stitching fewer embroidery threads are used anyway.)

You will soon discover with which *thread count* (number of warp and weft threads per centimetre or inch) you feel happiest. One of the best selections of different thread counts is that offered by the Danish

> *For that really* professional *touch, remember — when making up a cross-stitch piece — carefully* to press *it at each stage of construction*

Fabric should always be cut with warp threads vertical. Selvedges should be at the sides

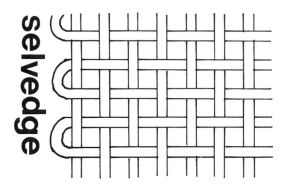

Handcraft Guild. Some of their fabrics have a *low* thread count – which means fewer and *larger* cross stitches (good if your eyesight is not 100%!). You can find the Guild's address in the list of suppliers at the back of the book.

Always *cut your fabric* with the warp threads vertical to you. The fabric's selvedge should therefore be vertical to the left and/or right sides of your fabric shape. Try and cut the shape exactly following a warp or weft thread. If you have problems cutting a straight line, slightly 'pull' or even completely 'extract or withdraw' the thread along the line you are going subsequently to cut.

As well as linens, there are of course *other fabrics* on which you can stitch – you will find a choice of more unusual materials in Chapter 7, 'Beyond cross stitch'. More usual alternatives to Glenshee and other evenweave linens include:

Aida (above) and Hardanger

Aida – 100% cotton fabric characterised by quartets of warp and weft threads woven tightly together so that 4 warp and 4 weft threads form an easily discernible 'block'. The fabric is usually 150 cm (42 in) wide with, typically, 4 or 6 'blocks' per cm: the more blocks per cm the softer the feel of the fabric. Cross stitches are generally worked over *1 block* of fabric.
Hardanger – another 100% cotton fabric, characterised by pairs of warp and weft threads woven together. The fabric is generally 150 cm (42 in) wide, with 9 pairs of warp and weft threads per cm. Cross stitches can be worked over *2, 3 or more pairs* of threads.

If you want the *most complete array of unusual threads* you should consider investing in Kay Montclare's *Fabric and Thread Collection* (available from World in Stitches, address at the back of this book). This thick, loose-leaf notebook is filled with fabric and thread swatches and is continually updated.

Before you do any stitching it is necessary to *bind the edges of your linen to prevent fraying or unravelling*. Temporary binding can be done in several ways. You may have access to a commercial tape-binding machine. If not, I find that two strips of narrow masking tape, half extending beyond the fabric and ironed and pressed with sticky sides together hold better than one wider strip folded over. You can also work hand or machine zigzag stitching or machine overlocking.

You might prefer to work a permanent binding around your linen. This will save later labour if, for instance, you are making a placemat. You can *mitre* all four corners as described and illustrated:

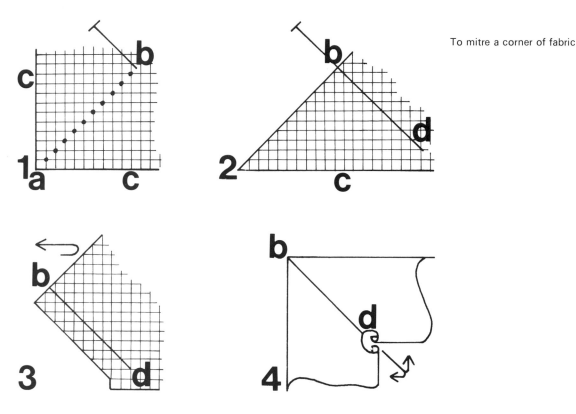

To mitre a corner of fabric

To mitre corners of your fabric:

1 Decide how deep you want your hem – say 8 threads. To allow extra for the 'turn under', count thread junctions diagonally from the corner (A), on the wrong side of the fabric, and insert a pin at the hem distance (say 8 threads) and extra 'turn under' (say 2 threads). In other words, after 10 junctions (B) fold the fabric, right sides together, so that C meets C.

2 Using sewing thread the same colour as the linen, hand sew tiny back stitches diagonally from B down 8 junctions (B-D).

3 Cut off most of the surplus fabric as shown. Turn the fabric right side out.

4 Fold under 'turn under' and hemstitch around.

Don't worry too much if you *accidentally snip through the fabric* when you are working cross stitch. You can hide the cut by working small darnings on the wrong side of the fabric (shaded, illustration 2). Cross stitches are then worked over the cut, on the right side, in the usual manner (3).

How to disguise an accidental snip in your fabric

1   **2**   **3**

Needles

Since threads are worked in the holes between warp and weft threads it is important not to pierce those threads.

Cross stitch is therefore traditionally worked with a blunt-ended needle. My favourite, when working on Glenshee linen, is a 'Tapestry 24', but if you are new to cross stitch and if you are not blessed with the best eyesight I suggest you start with a Tapestry size 20 or 22.

The most important thing is to have a needle with which you feel *comfortable*. It must be blunt ended, as mentioned. It should have an eye large enough for you to 'thread' and yet at the same time the main shaft must be narrow enough not to stretch the holes of your linen.

It is a good idea, incidentally, to have several needles. They have a knack of falling out of the linen and becoming irretrievably lost. One aid to finding temporarily 'lost' needles is always to *leave a needle threaded*. The thread of the 'lost' needle then catches your eye when you are looking for it.

Another tip I like to share with my students is that if you thread a needle by *licking* (i.e. the end of the thread), either cut that licked end off or pull it so that it is at the long end of the thread and straightaway held firmly on the reverse of the fabric. This avoids possible marking of the right side of the fabric.

(And of course I NEVER let my students park unthreaded – or threaded – needles between their lips. One of these days I am sure someone will swallow one.)

Having difficulty remembering in which direction your 'upper diagonal' should face? Refer constantly to the 'symbolic key' temporarily stitched in an upper corner of your fabric

Threads

Most of the projects in this book were worked with what is known as *stranded cotton* or *floss*, a highly versatile thread with six loosely-woven shiny strands. Embroidery can be worked with 1, 2, 3, 4, 5 or all the strands. From a purely economic viewpoint it is easier to try to work with 1, 2, 3 or 6 strands.

One of the advantages of using a stranded cotton is the large number of different colours available. DMC (itself a brand name but sometimes used generically) has nearly 300, which include many different values of one colour which is useful for delicate shading.

The minimum number of colours you will need is one. The maximum is up to you!

How do you store your stranded cottons?

I have seen more messy, albeit colourful, disarrays of different stranded cottons than would fill a lifetime to sort out. There are, fortunately, several 'yarn holders' now available, especially on the American market. The simplest form is a ring binder with removable clear plastic inserts into which you tuck your skeins so that they can be easily seen and removed when required.

My method is adapted from those clear-front display cabinets, with low drawers divided into lots of little compartments, each the length of a thread skein. If you purchase a clear-fronted tool or household supplies cabinet, with drawers and interior dividers that you fix as required, you can easily make your own display cabinet.

How do you extract a length of thread?

Stranded cottons are packed in 8 m (8¾ yd) skeins, held by paper bands. One of the threads should slightly protrude. *Do not remove the skein's paper bands.* Hold the skein in one hand and with the other gently pull the extending thread and cut off a required length. I usually sew with a length about *38 cm (15 in)*.

Some people find they get stranded cotton skeins into a messy 'knot' when trying carefully to extract a length. You might find it easier to unwrap the skein and wind the thread. One easy way is to cut a piece of strong card, say 38 cm (15 in) long. Unwrap the whole skein and wind the thread around the board. Cut the wound thread at each end of the board – and you have prepared lengths exactly 38 cm (15 in) long.

Before you stitch you should always '*strip*' your thread. Regardless of how many strands you will be using you should carefully pull out one thread and then another and another so that you have separated them all. When you put them back together – 2, 3 or as many strands as required – you will find you have untwisted stitches that better 'cover' the fabric.

Stranded cotton has no nap (as does woollen yarn). It does not matter therefore from which end you stitch.

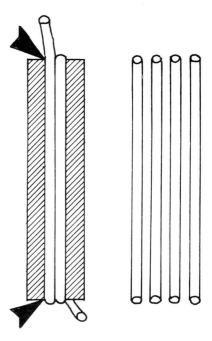

To prepare threads of equal length you can wind the thread around a shape (shaded) and snip at both ends (arrowed)

Before stitching with stranded cotton you should 'strip'. Extract one strand (1). This may cause a bunching of remaining strands which should be smoothed by a downward stroking (2). Other strands are similarly extracted and the required number laid together for smoother stitching (3)

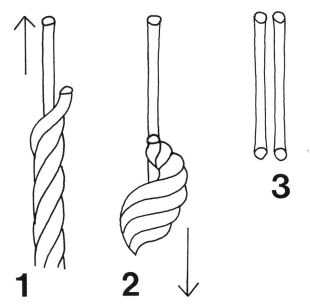

Among the *other threads* that people use is the Danish Handcraft Guild's *Dansk blomstergarn*, 'Danish flower thread'. This is a naturally-dyed linen thread available in nearly a hundred subtle shades. It is a two-ply thread which is stitched one ply at a time or with both as a pair (in which case do NOT strip). Each skein has a single paper band. Take it off and untwist the folded-double-and-twisted skein. If you cut both ends of the skein – 56 cm (22 in) when opened out – you will find that you have convenient lengths that long.

Scissors

You need at least two pairs of scissors for cross stitch work. A good sharp pair of dressmaking scissors is necessary for cutting out your fabric and a pair of small and handy scissors with sharply-pointed blades is best for snipping thread lengths and ends.

Most cross-stitchers have favourite scissors that are indispensable to their working. I find my orange-handled Fiskars (Wilkinsons) scissors are light and portable – and they can easily be seen (essential since I do so much stitching when travelling).

If you are worried about losing your scissors, even momentarily, you might like to tie a length of ribbon through both handles and hang the ribbon up on a hook near your favourite chair. Alternatively you can hang the scissors round your neck on a long ribbon. Do make sure, wherever you keep them, that your scissors are *near to hand*. Nothing is more infuriating than having to go and look for them. And if you don't interrupt yourself and carry on working without cutting off the end of that last thread you used you may get a tangle of surplus 'ends' on the back of your work which could even be pulled through to the front by subsequent threads.

Your favourite chair

Left-handed? Place the book in front of a mirror to be able to follow the stitch diagrams

I was first introduced to this phrase during a television exercise workout programme on a Florida T.V: station ('hold on to your favourite chair and take the first ballet position . . .').

This is what I have had for my embroidery all along! I actually have several favourite chairs. When I am in my studio I like to sit on my office chair pulled up to my large desk conveniently positioned by the window so that I can look up our (remarkably steep) garden as I sew. I can also stitch my best when in one (and one particular) chair in our living room. And one end of my mother-in-law's sofa is best when I am at her house. . . .

What does this mean? I think it illustrates that you *need to feel comfortable, at ease, to stitch your best.* The ideal 'stitching seat' is one that you find (a) comfortable, (b) handy and (c) well lit. It may be an upright, it may be a stool, it may even be a bed (as I usually find when staying in hotels). . . . It is up to you and where you are. What and wherever it is, however, I cannot stress too strongly the importance of being *at ease* when you stitch.

Good Light

When did you last have your eyes tested? A personal question this – but it is surprising how many people cannot remember and in fact do need to have their eyes tested.

Cross stitch work does require the best eyesight you can give it. That is not to say that those with poor vision cannot cross stitch. But be fair to cross stitch. Work with your *best eyesight* and in the *best light.*

As far as that light is concerned, a good direct beam from a directional lamp is generally best. You may agree with me that even extra-powerful overhead strips do not provide as good a light and they can be hard on the eyes, thus possibly producing headaches.

If you have not got a professional standing lamp, with ring light and central magnifier, I suggest you project an ordinary standing, table or spot lamp with a 100-watt bulb so that it shines in front of you, just above your knees, as you sit in your favourite chair.

☆☆☆☆☆☆☆☆☆☆☆

So much for the 'basic essentials'. Among the other things you might need are art materials, to produce your own drawings and graphs, and at least one embroidery frame or hoop.

Graph Paper, Notebook and Pencil, Coloured Pens or Pencils

I suggest that graph paper with 20 squares per 5 cm (10 squares per inch) is easy on the eye and yet the squares are small enough for you to be able to get a lot of design on a fairly small area of paper.

I personally use graphed *tracing* paper. It is not widely available but you should be able to get it from your local art store.

You can, incidentally, use graphed tracing paper to *copy motifs in this book*. Make sure you have an appropriately-sized graph paper and lay it over the book's page, the trellis of the paper and the book in exact alignment. Then simply trace the design through.

1

2 green blue

Stitching from a graph or chart is much easier than you might fear. A simple blocked design (1) has a key with colour codes (2). Each graph square is subsequently converted as a stitch in the appropriate colour (3)

one stitch

3

Most people find it easier to follow *coloured graphs*. To avoid colouring the graphs in this book, you can make a tracing as described above and *colour the tracing*.

If you have never *stitched from a graph before* you will find it remarkably easy. Set the relevant graph as near to you as possible (you could stand the book in one of those clear lucite (perspex) cookbook stands). Follow carefully, converting each *square* on the graph into a *stitch* on your fabric. If, for instance, your graph has the symbol for a red square in the upper left hand corner, then similarly work a red cross stitch in what you want to be the upper left hand corner of your stitched design.

A few *tips for graph-following*:

1 You may find it easier to colour your graph with appropriate coloured pens or pencils; you can make a tracing and colour that, as I have already just suggested.

2 It is easier to stitch from a graph by working *a whole area* or part of an area in one colour and then proceeding to an *adjacent* block of another colour. Do not attempt to 'read off' horizontal lines in computer style. 'Visualise' a motif or area of a motif as you are stitching it.

3 If you are working a particularly complicated area of a design, it might be a help to lay a ruler or piece of paper over part of the graph to remind yourself *exactly* where you are (or should be).

Stranded cottons have no nap *so you can stitch from either end of your thread*

Frames or Hoops

One of the (many) advantages of cross stitching is that it CAN be hand-held. The natural linen threads of the fabric do not distort, as does a stiff 'sized' canvas when working what is known as 'canvaswork' or 'needle-point'. Tension is not complicated, as in drawn thread and other embroidery techniques which definitely do require a frame to hold the fabric taut.

I prefer working with the fabric held in my hand. I can thus 'stitch', making a needle entry and exit through the fabric in one movement.

If you feel happier, however, working on a frame, then do so. In this case you will probably 'stab', making one needle entry and then one needle exit through the fabric.

Linen threads do not easily 'mark' and if you do choose to work on a frame you can use a circular or oval 'hoop' frame. My favourite is a lightweight brown plastic hoop: I especially favour the 10 cm (4 in) diameter size which enables me to concentrate on just one small area of linen at a time.

If you use a hoop frame, the linen is held taut between the two rings of the frame. If you use a wooden hoop frame you might like to bind the wooden rings with bandage or tape to protect the fabric.

I do NOT suggest a square or rectangular frame on to which you have to pin or lace your linen. Not only might pins mark the linen but both pinning and lacing could pull the fabric irrevocably out of shape.

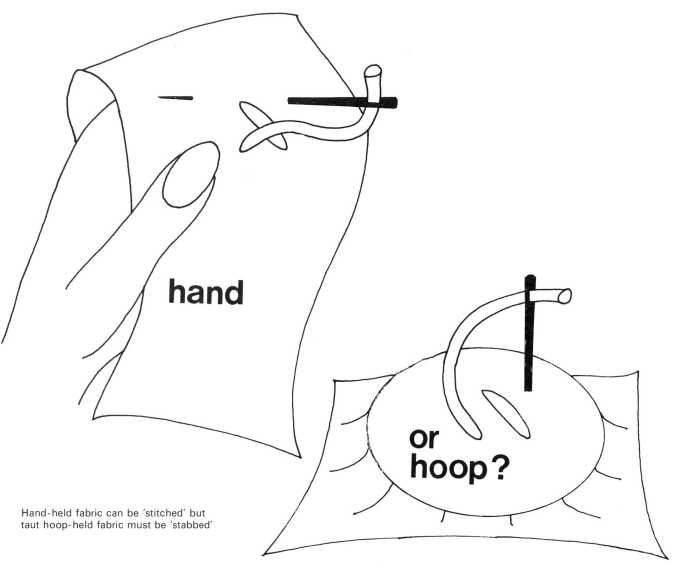

hand

or hoop?

Hand-held fabric can be 'stitched' but taut hoop-held fabric must be 'stabbed'

Pre-stitch Hints

Even advanced embroiderers sometimes miscount and it is better to prevent rather than cure. . . . Things I find helpful before starting to cross stitch include:

1 *Dividing the fabric into quadrants* to find the centre of my area. I use a pale blue or similar pale-coloured sewing thread to work tackings (bastings) from top to bottom, marking the half way, and similarly bisecting the height, from side to side of the fabric. I leave the tackings in until I have finished all my cross stitching.

2 *Making my symbolic 'key'* to remind me myself which diagonal should

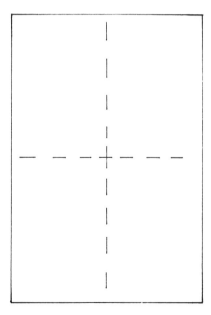

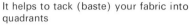

It helps to tack (baste) your fabric into quadrants

It also helps to stitch a large symbolic cross as a 'key' to the direction of subsequent cross stitches. The key is later removed

be uppermost. Even the most advanced stitcher, in her enthusiasm, sometimes makes a mistake and crosses a stitch in the wrong direction. To help avoid this, I suggest that before you start any proper stitching you work a *large token cross stitch* over six or as many threads as you like (no matter what size your eventual stitches will be). Work it in the top right hand corner if you are right handed: work it in the top left hand corner if you are left handed. Constantly glance at your 'key' as you subsequently stitch to make sure that your cross stitches are all worked in similar manner. (Note: this 'key' is only temporary: remember to remove it – and your quadrant tackings, when you finish your main cross stitching.)

How do you *start and finish* stitching with a length of thread? Well, it is important to remember that although perfectionists today require maximum neatness on the reverse of a finished piece of work, in the past many cross stitch pieces were worked with the intention of only being viewed from the front. Therefore traditionally it is not *essential* to make the reverse of your work faultless.

You may however like to keep the reverse as neat as possible and you should certainly avoid having excess ends of thread hanging loose.

Among the many methods of starting a new length of thread are:

1 Work one or two minute back or running stitches on the area of linen that will immediately be covered by the first cross stitches you will work with the new thread. These stitches will therefore completely cover the holding back or running stitches.

2 The '*waste knot*' method. As the illustration shows, make a firm knot at

Don't forget to strip (the thread, that is). Pull out one strand and then another and lay as many strands together to achieve smoother, untwisted stitching

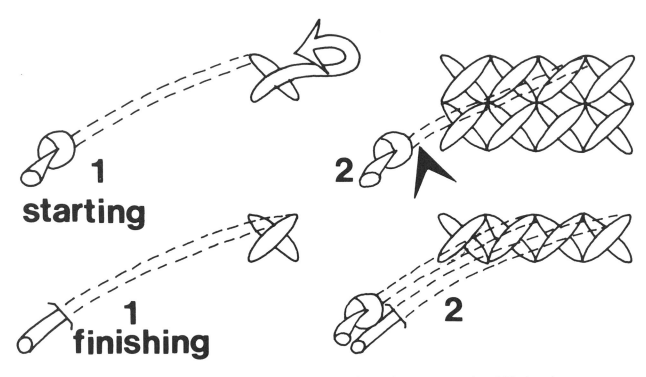

The waste knot method can be used to start a new thread. The knot is cut as arrowed. Similarly a waste tail can be used to finish a thread. This is stitched in with the next thread's starting knot

the end of the thread. From the front of the linen, make a long stitch (here dotted) *from* the direction in which you will subsequently work cross stitches. These stitches will hold the first long stitch and then you can cut off (i.e. 'waste') the knot.

3 If you prefer, you can secure a new thread with one or two little holding stitches on the reverse, worked as weavings in and out of stitches already worked. (I should point out, however, that reverse weavings distort the front of stitches already worked.)

When you are finishing a thread you must similarly secure it and you can use corresponding methods:

1 Make one or two small holding back or running stitches in the direction in which you will be stitching with your next thread.

2 As illustrated, make a 'waste tail', the corresponding holding method to the 'waste knot'. Take the tail *to* the area you will next be covering with stitching. You will find that the tail does not need knotting: it will stay of its own accord, and will be bound at the same time as the waste knot of the next thread by that thread's first few stitches.

3 Weave in and out of the reverse of stitches already worked. (This method is not recommended for the reasons set out above.)

And So to Cross Stitch . . .

As its name implies, cross stitch looks like a diagonal cross. Actually the name is a misnomer, for as you will see it is formed of *two* stitches, diagonals which bisect each other, usually at right angles.

You can work a diagonal up to the right and cross it with one up to the left. Alternatively you can work a diagonal up to the left and cross it with one up to the right. . . .

Should the upper diagonals go up to the left or up to the right?

Personally I would say that this is a matter for you to choose. Do whatever comes naturally . . . but stick to it, for the ONLY hard-and-fast rule (unless you are emulating embroideries from other particular parts of the globe) is that *all your upper diagonals should face the same direction*.

In my historical and ethnographic studies I have found no overall consistency. Some stitchers worked/work 'up to the right' and others worked/work 'up to the left'. I always stitch up to the right.

Choose the direction you prefer – and stick to it.

There are many different ways of *forming a series of cross stitches*.

You may prefer to work a line of stitches in two stages. To begin with you form the first diagonals, from one end of the line to the other. Then, on the return journey, you work all the upper diagonals. You can form horizontal or vertical lines of stitches in this manner. If you are working a horizontal row you will normally work from right to left if you are right-handed, and from left to right if you are left-handed.

There are however many *advantages in working a line of COMPLETE stitches*. If I am working a horizontal line of stitches I work the whole line in one stage, with one complete stitch followed by another stitch right next to it, and then another and so on. I form vertical lines in the same manner. The advantages of working a line of complete stitches include:

1 It is easier not to miscount fabric threads if you work whole rather than half stitches.

2 I have found from experience that working a line of half stitches followed by a superimposed line of the other half of the stitches can result in what I call 'slipped' stitches, which look extremely unsightly and unprofessional.

3 It is easier to unpick whole (rather than two half) stitches! If you unpick a line of whole stitches you only have to make small snips through each upper diagonal, on the right side of the fabric. Whole stitches can then easily be removed with a needle, scissors end or tweezers. (By contrast, if you unpick a line of half-and-then-half stitches you have completely to remove the line of upper diagonals before laboriously taking out the line of lower diagonals.)

One point that should be stressed is that neighbouring stitches should *share a hole*. One arm and one leg of a stitch should be worked into the

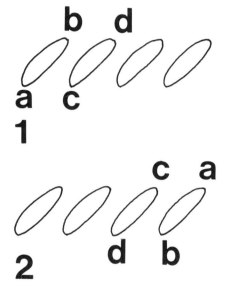

It doesn't matter if you work from left to right (1) or from right to left (2) . . .

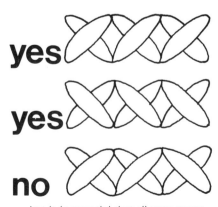

. . . but it *is* essential that all your upper diagonals face the same direction

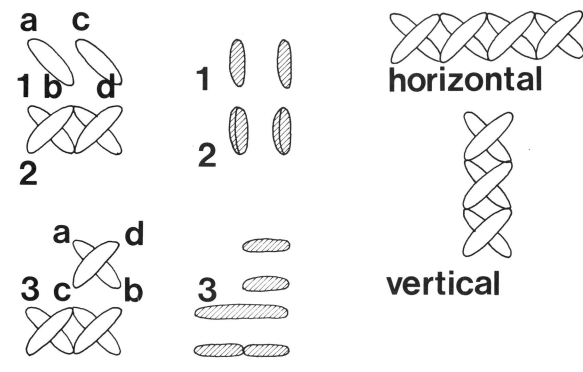

Some people prefer to work several half-crosses (1) topped by half-crosses in the other direction (2). Others, myself included, favour working one complete cross stitch followed by another complete stitch (3). The stitches as they appear on the reverse of the fabric are shown shaded

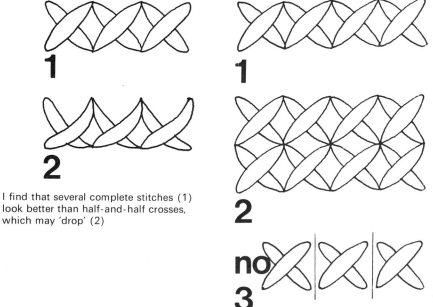

I find that several complete stitches (1) look better than half-and-half crosses, which may 'drop' (2)

Neighbouring stitches (1) and neighbouring lines (2) should share common holes. No fabric threads should be left between stitches (3)

same hole of fabric as one arm and one of the adjacent stitch (if on the same alignment). Similarly, if you are working one horizontal row of stitches above another horizontal row of stitches, then arms of a stitch should share a hole with the legs of the stitch immediately above, and its legs should share a common hole with arms of the stitch below.

What size cross stitches?

My own preference is towards stitches over 2 warp and 2 weft threads of fabric. But you can stitch over 2, 3, 4 or more, just as you – and your eyesight – feel happiest. Once again, choose which size stitches you want and, at any rate within the same part of one design, *be consistent.*

If you are not sure which size stitches suit you best, work little sample blocks, one with rows of stitches over 2 threads, one over 3 threads and one over 4 threads.

Contrary to most sceptical opinion cross stitch can also be worked over *one thread* of fabric. If you want to try this, follow the illustrations here to form, first of all, a line of alternate first diagonals. On the return journey, work the other first diagonals. Then make a second journey, forming upper diagonals of alternate stitches on the outward excursion and the remaining upper diagonals on the return.

To prevent cross stitches worked over only 1 fabric thread from 'slipping', work alternate half cross stitches (1) and fill in interstices (2). Similarly form the upper diagonals in two stages (3).

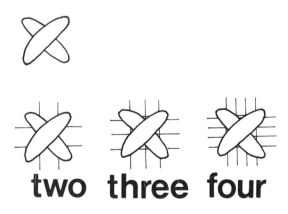

two three four

You can work cross stitches over as many fabric threads as you like

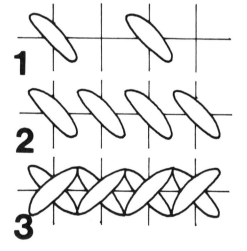

Confidence with basic stitching is essential before you progress to some of the experimental forms set out later in the book. (Yes, you CAN work on canvas; yes, you CAN leave threads between stitches if you want; yes, you CAN break all the rules . . . !).

First, however, I suggest you perfect CONFIDENCE in your ability to produce exact and easy cross stitches.

If you are a real beginner try these simple 'steps in confidence':

1 Prepare (i.e. cut, bind and mark quadrants – see p. 20) an area of fabric about 25.4 cm (10 in) square and thread up 2 strands of stripped stranded cotton. Form a symbolic cross in the upper right hand corner (left, if you are left handed).

2 Using any method of securing the end of the thread, and starting stitching 5 cm (2 in) down and 5 cm (2 in) in from the right hand edge of your fabric, work 10 cross stitches (over 2, 3 or 4 threads – but be consistent), remembering – if you are right-handed – that:
(a) you are working from right to left
(b) neighbouring stitches share common holes
(c) all your upper diagonals must face the same direction as your symbolic stitch.

3 After you have worked 10 cross stitches, secure your length of thread and cut off the end. Work another line of 10 stitches about 2.5 cm (1 in) below the first line. Immediately beneath this line work a second line of 10 stitches: neighbouring stitches of this second line share holes and also all upper arms of these stitches share holes with the legs of the stitches above. Similarly work a third line of 10 stitches immediately beneath the second line.

4 If you are happy with the two blocks (one with 1 and one with 2 lines of stitches) that you have worked, try following a simple graph. Look at the alphabets on pp. 86–8 and pick out the initial of your family name in any one of the scripts shown. Making sure that you do not begin stitching too close to the edge of your fabric, try stitching that initial. Remember, it is not at this stage imperative that the reverse of your work looks as neat as the front. Strive for familiarity not only in following the graph but also in working first one cross stitch above another, then a stitch next to that one and then perhaps 'jumping' diagonally to the next stitch. Make sure that all your upper diagonals face the same way.

Do you feel happy with what you have done?

If not, try the same three-stage exercise all over again, using differently coloured threads and choosing another initial. If you DO feel happy, then try some of the more simple motifs diagrammed in the book. Experiment and work a 'sampler', a 'test-piece' of different stitch formations.

And you might like to try some of the *more common cross stitch variations*.

If you particularly want the reverse of your work to look neat for instance, you might like to experiment with one of the *marking stitches* often used in the past for initialling and numbering household linens of which the reverse would show. Three forms of marking stitch are illustrated. All finish up as crosses on the front. On the reverse, one shows neatly-formed box shapes and the others are '*two-sided*', with crosses on this facet as well as the front.

You might like to try *portions of cross stitch*. The first stitches I have already introduced you to have been perfectly-formed stitches with four equally long arms and legs. On your cross stitch sampler, work one or two half stitches – in other words, just the first diagonals. And try working some 'three-quarter' cross stitches, which look as if one arm or leg has been left out or amputated.

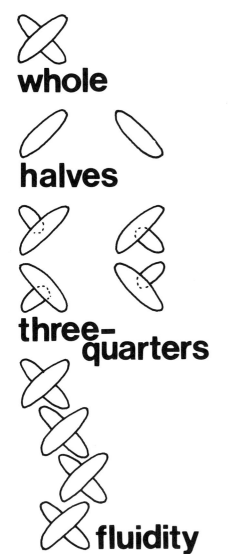

whole

halves

three-quarters

fluidity

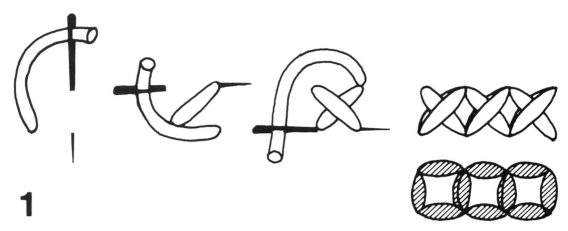

1

One form of marking cross stitch produces square boxes (shaded) on the reverse

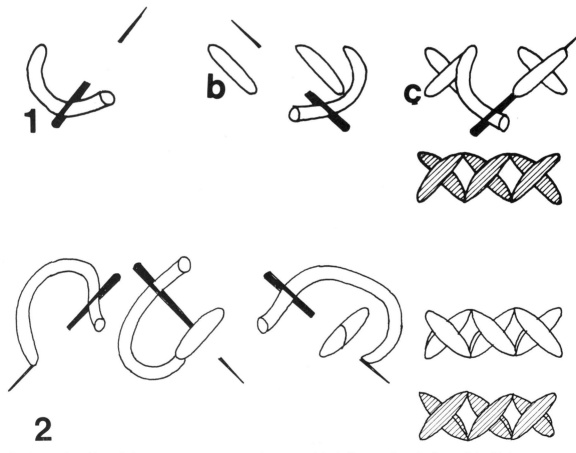

2

Two other forms of marking stitches appear as crosses on the reverse (shaded) as well as the front of the fabric

Try some *fluid cross stitching*. Work a horizontal or vertical row of stitches that purposely do NOT share common holes. Set one stitch one thread up or over or down from its neighbour. . . .

EXPERIMENT . . . Remember that cross stitching should be *fun*. . . .

☆☆☆☆☆☆☆☆☆☆

There are so many different forms of cross stitch, You might like to try, for instance, *Italian cross stitch*, alternatively called 'arrowhead cross stitch' or 'two-sided Italian stitch'. It looks especially good when several rows are worked. Notice how each cross is contained in a box. Another *boxed stitch* is *diagonal cross stitch*, which has upright crosses. (Remember how I said earlier that all, well nearly all, cross stitch rules can be broken?).

Cross stitch forms

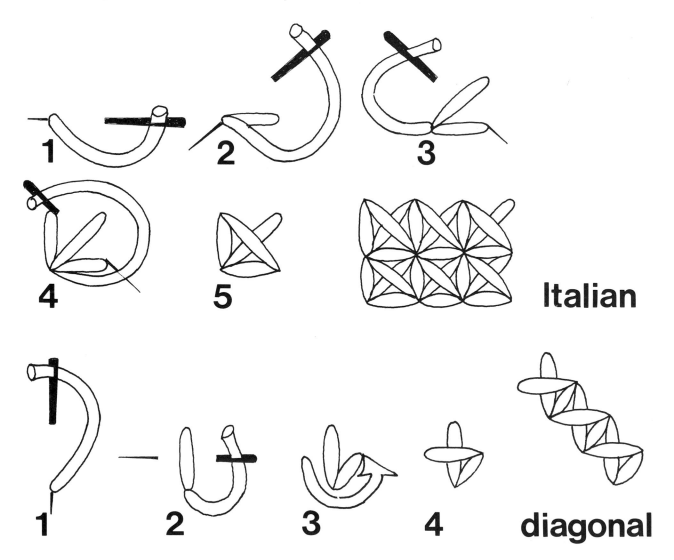

Cross stitch can be *combined* with some of the other basic techniques. *Chained cross stitch* is, as its name implies, a combination of chain and cross stitches.

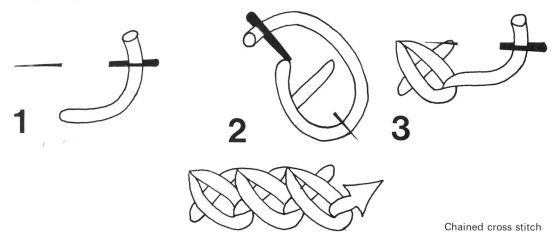

Chained cross stitch

Cross stitches with *differently-lengthed diagonals* can be worked as an interlaced line to form *long-legged cross stitch*, also known as 'long-armed cross stitch'. This is a particularly useful technique that can be worked flat or formed *over* the edge of a piece, as a firm edge binding (the master of what she specifically calls 'binding stitch' is the American designer and author Joan Young – her booklets *Miracles with the binding stitch*, *More miracles with the binding stitch* and *Miraculous handbags and totes* are all available from Young at Heart, 1518 Spruce Drive, Kalamazoo, Mi 49008, USA). Other forms of differently-lengthened-diagonal stitches include *Montenegrin stitch*, *basket stitch* and *herringbone stitch*.

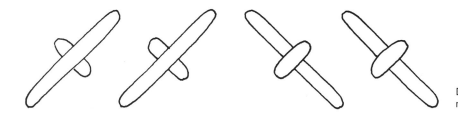

Diagonals of a cross stitch need not necessarily be the same length

By contrast, forms of *concentrated* cross stitches can form bars or such blocks as *crow's foot* or *sprat's head*, useful as dressmaking stitches as they securely hold, say, the top of a skirt's slit to prevent tearing.

Cross stitches can form a *reverse* design. In *Assisi work*, for instance, the motif is left unworked and the reserves, areas around, are stitches, typically, in one colour of close long-legged cross stitch.

Cross stitches can be *embellished* (decorated). You can work two superimposed cross stitches to form *double cross stitch*. Four small extra stitches crossing a cross stitch's arms and legs produce *rice stitch*, also known as 'crossed-corners cross stitch'.

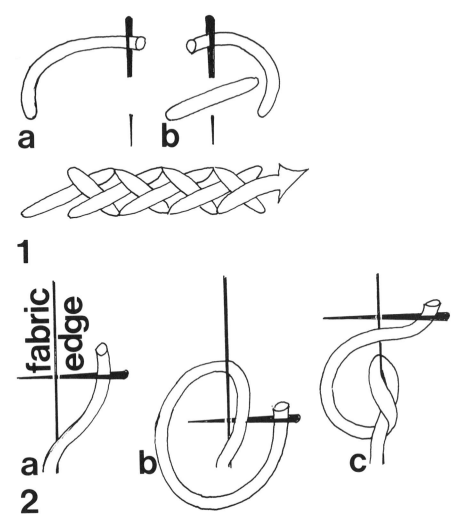

1

2

Long-legged cross stitch (1) can be worked over the edge of a piece as a binding stitch (2)

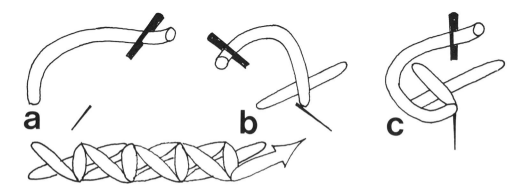

Montenegrin cross stitch

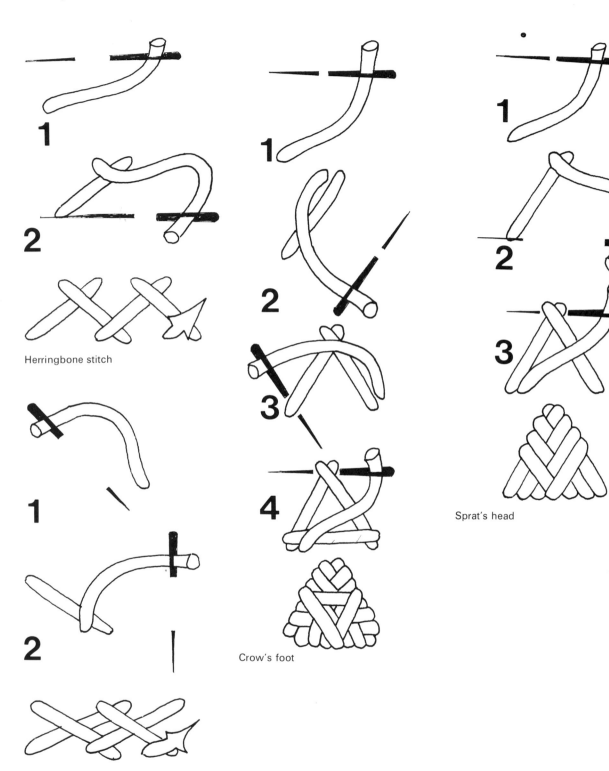

1

2

Herringbone stitch

1

2

Basket stitch

1

2

3

4

Crow's foot

1

2

3

Sprat's head

double

rice

Embellished cross stitches

You will find many other cross stitch forms elsewhere in the book: special 'national' stitches are shown in the international chapter, for instance. Here I have discussed only BASIC knowledge.

You can now do cross stitch. If you want to learn about designing you might like to turn directly to Chapter 4. If you want specific projects with all making up details look up 'Projects' in the index. If you feel like more experiments turn to Chapter 7. If, on the other hand, you would prefer to spend a few moments reading about the history of cross stitch and learning about fascinating designs from all over the world, I suggest you simply turn the page and carry on reading.

2 Cross stitch history

Although, as I have said, cross stitch is described as 'the most popular of all embroidery stitches', zealous historians have not, despite delving into records, archives and archaeological sites, succeeded in discovering the moment, and place, of its creation.

One of my favourite books is the comprehensive *Art of embroidery* by Marie Schuette and Sigrid Müller-Christensen (Thames & Hudson, 1964, English translation by Donald King). Its earliest illustration is a chain and stem stitch Hellenistic fragment dating from the fourth to fifth century: the first *cross stitch* piece is possibly Coptic, seventh to eighth century (Victoria & Albert Museum, 814–1903). Even in this example – a roundel (circular panel), 17.5 cm (6¾ in) diameter, with an outer floral border encompassing a rendering of the Visitation – cross stitch has to share its glory with satin and split stitching and with couched work.

Thereafter many of the cross stitch pieces illustrated come from Germany. There is a mid-thirteenth century altar frontal from the Convent of Heiningen, in Lower Saxony. This marvellous work, now in Kloster St Marienberg, Helmstedt, measures 106 × 236 cm (41¾ × 93 in) and shows Christ in Glory flanked by five saints standing in realistic-looking arches. An inscription names Hildeswit and Walburgis, who had established the convent in the time of Otto III (980–1002).

Germany, especially Westphalia, was also one of the main production areas for long-legged cross stitch; a Westphalian box cover can be seen, for instance, in the Kunstgewerbemuseum in Berlin (their number 88.651). It was also popular in Iceland, where mediaeval motifs were worked on large wall hangings, sometimes 10 m (11 yd) long, as in the case of a sixteenth century piece from Hof, in the North of the island (Nationalmuseum, Copenhagen, CCCLXXI).

Perhaps travellers brought knowledge of the various possibilities of the cross stitch family to England, for the main introduction to the British Isles appeared at that time of a flowering of international travel and trade, the reign of Elizabeth I. One of the best-known early English examples is a sixteenth-century purse, 10.8 cm (4¼ in) square (V&A 244–1896).

The tradition of domestic embroidery, worked both by amateurs (in this instance gentlewomen) for the purpose of decorating their own homes and by professionals (generally men) for decorating the houses of others, began at this time. And so as a corollary did the whole exciting field of canvas work evolve.

Assisi work piece, with the motifs left unstitched and surrounds worked. 15.24×52 cm (6×20½ in). *(V&A. 73–1901)*

Elizabethan houses were cold and draughty. Canvas work bed hangings and valances, carpets – at that time usually covers for tables and open-shelved 'cupboards' – and long rectangular cushion covers for benches and window seats were easily portable and provided protection against the elements.

I should explain at this point that 'canvas work' is, quite simply, any work *on canvas*. Confusingly, today it is widely known, especially in America, as 'needlepoint', which is technically a needle-made lace, or 'needlepoint tapestry', wrongly implying a woven decoration.

Whereas today we distinguish between 'evenweave', usually a soft fabric, and 'canvas', a rigid construction, sometimes heavily sized, the term 'canvas' is used in historic terms to mean any evenweave material with recognisable holes between warp and weft threads. The 'canvas' of the sixteenth century is therefore not dissimilar to our 'evenweave' of today. It was stitched with woollen or silk threads, the latter usually from the Levant. Cross stitch, sometimes known as 'gros point', was popular, as was the half cross known as 'petit point' or 'tent stitch' (now the main purely-canvas technique). Cross was the senior stitch: half cross was widely used later in the century.

Many of the designs stitched were floral, with motifs taken from herbals such as *La clef des champs*, by Jacques le Moyne, published in 1586. (There is a comprehensive list of herbals and garden books published throughout the sixteenth century in George Wingfield Digby's *Elizabethan Embroidery*, Faber, 1963, p. 44.) Other popular motifs included real and extraordinary animals, birds and water creatures, sometimes adapted from the volumes by a Zurich doctor, Conrad Gesner, which were published together as one under the title *Historia animalium* in 1560. (You can see rendering of some of Gesner's designs in *Curious Woodcuts of Fanciful and Real Beasts*, published by Dover Publications Inc. in 1971.)

In some cases, instead of embellishing a large area of canvas, embroiderers preferred to work smaller bits which were subsequently applied – put on – to another area.

Particularly after the Dissolution of the Monasteries and nunneries

from 1539, a large number of rich vestments had been sold to secular hands and cut up to form, say, wall hangings. Since counted thread embellishment was not possible on finely-woven brocades and other silks, embellishment had to be provided by embroidered bits of canvas applied to those fabrics.

The best known of all such appliqué hangings must surely be the 'Oxburgh hangings', called after the National Trust house in Cambridge-shire where complete panels can be seen: other appliqué motifs from the set are displayed in the Victoria & Albert Museum.

Mary Queen of Scots (1542–87) is thought to have worked some of the square, octagonal and cruciform canvas appliqué motifs during the 18 years of her imprisonment, from 1569, at the hands of her cousin Elizabeth, whose crown she claimed. (See Margaret Swain's *The Needlework of Mary Queen of Scots*, Van Nostrand Reinhold, 1973, for a detailed description of the panels known to have been worked by the Scottish queen.) Some of the other pieces were probably worked by the wife of her 'guardian', the Earl of Shrewsbury. Better known as 'Bess of Hardwick' (see David Durant's *Bess of Hardwick*, Weidenfeld & Nicol-

One of the panels thought to have been worked by Bess of Hardwick (*c.* 1520–1608). The initials are hers (Elizabeth, Countess of Shrewsbury). Cross-stitch panel 38 cm (nearly 15 in) across, hemmed to brown velvet. (*National Trust*)

son, 1977), Bess had several embroiderers working for her, usually men who were part of her household. Her embroiderers drew designs for Bess' clothes and stitched them, and when not so employed they might have worked on cushion covers and larger pieces. We know, too, that an upholsterer called Florens Broshere often stitched backgrounds of designs, thus leaving the more exciting main motifs to the needles of the ladies of the household.

Another fine example of Bess of Hardwick's commissioned (if not her own) work is provided by a magnificent folding screen still to be seen at the home she so opulently built as soon as the Earl of Shrewsbury, her fourth husband, died in 1590. The screen has 30 octagonal canvaswork applications, all with similar decoration and all but two of them bearing Bess's initials, 'ES'. With the exception of one panel inscribed *Virtutis praemium* ('reward of virtue'), all bear Latin proverbs from Erasmus, and the central area of each panel is formed of a plant adapted from Pietro Andrea Mattioli's *Herbal*, published in Lyon in 1572.

Allowing for what would today be considered atrocious communications, the fact that Bess of Hardwick at some time in the last quarter of the sixteenth century at least organised the working of 30 cross stitch panels with designs taken from a work published a few years before in southern France shows that cross stitchers have traditionally been *quick to follow new ideas and trends* in other designs and art fields than merely their own. . . .

It will already be obvious that the history of cross stitch in the West is associated from the start with household and other decoration rather than with clothing embellishment. By contrast, it will be seen in the next chapter that ethnographic cross stitch is involved in both clothing AND other decoration.

The genealogy of cross stitching in the West must here be mentioned. After the plethora of cross stitch worked in preceding decades the technique lost popularity at the end of the sixteenth century. Its close younger relation, the half cross 'tent stitch', rose to become the main counted thread form of the seventeenth century.

Fortunately for the cross stitch historian, however, the technique continued on samplers, worked on small areas of what is generally known in sampler terminology merely as linen.

There are many excellent books on samplers available. If you are specifically interested in the sampler aspect of cross stitch I recommend you to the following works:

Pamela Clabburn, *Samplers*, Shire Publications, 1977

Dorothea Kay, *Embroidered Samplers*, Scribner's, 1979

Donald King, *Samplers*, HMSO, 1960

Glee J. Krueger, *A Gallery of American Samplers: the Theodore H. Kapnek Collection*, E. P. Dutton, 1978

Philadelphia Museum of Art, *The Story of Samplers*

Sampler worked by Mary Elliot in 1736: as well as cross stitch and two-sided Italian cross stitch, chain, satin, herringbone, eyelet, outline and stem stitches have been used. The silk-on-linen piece measures 43.8×20.9 cm (17¼×8¼ inches). (*V&A T.22–1940 Q.41C*)

Left: Flowers on organdie really personalize this lingerie pouch

Below: A simple geometric cross stitch motif enlivens a plain linen place mat

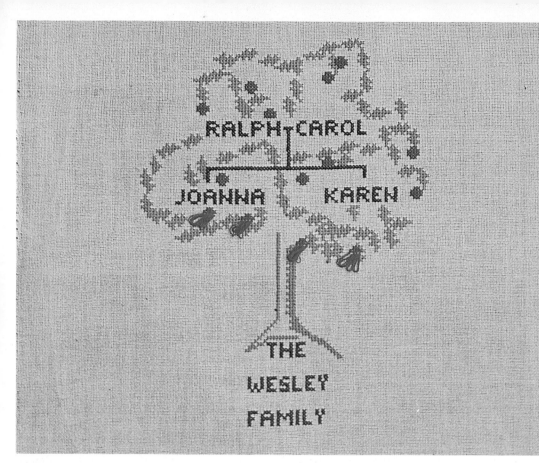

RALPH — CAROL

JOANNA   KAREN

THE

WESLEY

FAMILY

Left: You too can stitch a family tree!

Bottom left: A young man with his Humpty Dumpty cross stitch sweater

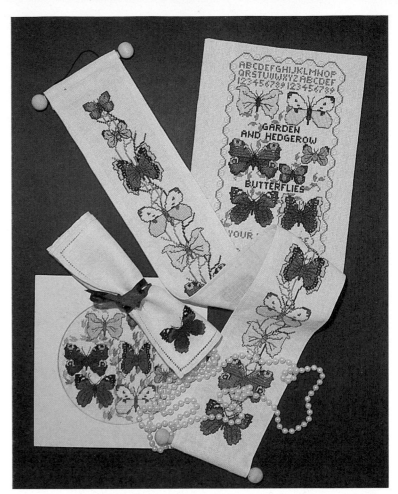

Right: Butterflies, all fully diagrammed in the book, can be worked singly or grouped in many different formations

Below: The calico apron and headscarf

Left: Cross stitch can be combined with other techniques

Below: A traditional middle-eastern open robe with decoration mainly on the front yoke and sleeves

Anne Sebba, *Samplers*: *Five Centuries of a Gentle Craft*, Weidenfeld & Nicolson, 1979; Thames & Hudson, 1979

Naomi E. A. Tarrant, *Samplers*, Royal Scottish Museum, 1978.

Cross stitch is worked – albeit with other techniques – on the earliest known dated sampler (V&A T.190–1960), that signed and dated by Jane Bostocke in 1598. Although later samplers were often the work of children, this was probably by adult hands, and it might have been stitched to commemorate the birth of her sister Alice Lee, born two years before.

Jane Bostocke's sampler is notable not only for its age; with a 43 × 38 cm (17 × 15 in) format, it differs completely from the typical sampler of the next few years.

Seventeenth century samplers are distinguished by their long and narrow proportions – say 60 × 20 cm (24 × 8 in), or three times as tall as wide. Designs were often worked in horizontal bands worked to within a centimetre (under half an inch) of each side of the fabric, and with one band closely set above and below another so as not to waste any of the precious material.

I must stress that these early examples of English samplers are not exclusively cross stitch. A variety of techniques was employed; these samplers were test pieces of various stitches as well as of patterns.

By the mid eighteenth century samplers had less exaggerated proportions, say 33 × 22 cm (13 × 9 in), or a ratio of 3:2 of height to width. There were also square samplers, about 20 × 20 cm (8 × 8 in), so that the piece could conveniently be set into a frame. As well as linen, wool, sometimes 'tammy', or linsey-woolsey – which had linen warp and wool weft – were used.

Sometimes fewer different stitches were worked. Eight-year old Ann Body, for instance, stitched a sampler in 1789 simply in cross and two-sided cross stitches.

Poor little girl! I imagine her patiently stitching her complicated inscription:

> "*Dear mother I am young and cannot show*
> *Such work as I unto your goodness owe*
> *Be pleased to smile on this my small endeavour*
> *Ill strive to learn and be obedient ever*"

(V&A, T.292–1916).

At least by the end of the eighteenth century samplers were more often the work of children's hands. Young girls, either in schools or at home, perfected their alphabets as they patiently stitched various different scripts and letterings. As well as practising their stitching, they learnt such requisites of a well-brought up young lady as how to recognise the appropriate crown or coronet of a king, duke, marquis, earl, viscount or baron, motifs which might later be stitched on linen and under-wear belonging to their husbands – or to their employers if they were

Map sampler 'signed' by I. Toghill in 1787. Lettering is formed of cross stitches over one linen thread. The overall measurements are 30.48×24.1 cm (12×19½ in)

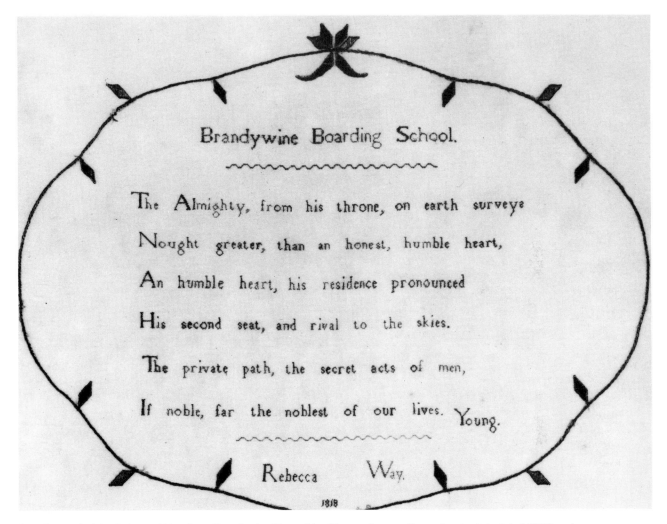

Sampler worked by Rebecca Way, from Brandywine Township, Chester County, Pennsylvania. It is dated 1818 and measures 28.6×33 cm (11¼×13 in). (*The Henry Francis du Pont Winterthur Museum. 59.1133*)

going into service.

Finished samplers provided visible proof to students' parents that work had been accomplished at school. Many schoolgirls' samplers purposely included motifs that might have warmed their mothers' hearts, such as houses or maps of the British Isles (not only out of patriotism but to illustrate geographical lessons).

America undoubtedly has one of the world's strongest traditions of cross-stitched samplers. The earliest examples were worked in New England, then in Pennsylvania and New Jersey. In America the sampler-making tradition was inspired by British and particularly Dutch heritage. Here schoolgirl samplers have been especially well documented. Samplers from the Westtown School, in Chester County, Pennsylvania, for instance, usually consist of a simple inscription enclosed in a black vine-and-leaf scroll border (see Margaret B. Schiffer's article 'Chester County

FAMILY REGISTER

John Flint son of Thomas and Lydia Flint Born at Nobleborough Feb⁺ 16 1774 Maried April 3 1800 to Lydia Norton Daughter of Ebene⁷ and Elizabeth Norton Born at Edgarton March 14 1779

PROGENY	BIRTHS	DEATHS
Sophia Flint	Janv⁺ 7 1801	Dec⁺ 20 1818
Elizabeth N. Flint	Nov 16 1802	
Lorenza Flint	Oct 28 1804	Dec 11 1818
Martha C. Flint	Jan 14 1807	
John P. Flint	Mar 17 1809	
Clarissa N. Flint	Nov 29 1811	
Mary R. Flint	Nov 22 1814	
Sophia L. Flint	June 22 1820	

American girls often worked family record samplers. This one records the family of John Flint, a trader in Bath, Maine. 93.9 × 70.1 cm (37¼ × 27½ in), framed. (*The Daughters of the American Revolution Museum: Gift of the Colonel Dummer Sewall DAR Chapter through Elwina Durgin*)

Samplers' in *Needlework: An Historical Survey*, edited by Betty Ring, Antiques Magazine Library, 1975, 74). The sixteenth student enrolled at the school, which opened in 1799, was Rebecca Bud, who later married John Comly, a teacher at the Pleasant Hill Boarding School in Byberry, Philadelphia County – and subsequently similarly designed samplers were worked in *that* establishment. By the middle of the eighteenth century some American samplers had landscapes along the bottom of their design. More and more recognizable buildings and scenes were recorded (see the view of St Patrick's Church, Baltimore, shown on Mary Ann Craft's 1822 piece, Daughters of the American Revolution Museum, D.C., 66.219). Another American specialty was the working of family record samplers such as that illustrated here. (There were also more sombre mourning samplers but they were generally not cross stitched.)

If, like me, you are fascinated by the background to samplers – who worked them, when and from where did the designs come? – you have years of enthralling study and interest ahead of you! Look out for the writings of those authors I have already mentioned – and also articles and books by Betty Ring, Susan Swann and Elisabeth Donaghy Garrett. Study the collections in the Victoria & Albert Museum (London), the Royal Scottish Museum (Edinburgh), The University of Kansas Museum of Art and the Daughters of the American Revolution Museum (D.C.). And subscribe to the relevant Christie's and Sotheby Parke Bernet's saleroom catalogues. You will always be learning.

✗✗✗✗✗✗✗✗✗✗

Meanwhile . . . while little girls stitched samplers, what were their elders up to?

The eighteenth century was the high point of cross stitched carpets, by now intended to lie on floors (some of the finest examples can be seen in The Henry Francis du Pont Winterthur Museum).

Most stitched furnishings at this time were – as they continued to be – executed in half-cross (tent) stitch, though in many cases cross stitched examples have survived the best as there are two layers of thread covering each stitched area.

Early in the nineteenth century adult needleworkers, ladies all and certainly not those who had to stitch for their living, became addicted to 'Berlin woolwork', counted thread stitchery copied from hand-coloured paper graphs originally published by a printseller in that city about 1804. As with cross stitch charts – or cookery recipes – today, the paper patterns were quickly passed from one embroiderer to another. Also, patterns were copiously produced – by 1840 it is estimated there were no less than 14,000 designs on the market. (Until 1842 there was no copyright law.)

Many of the Berlin woolwork addicts stitched small blocks of different patterns in brightly-coloured wools on long and narrow samplers, the edges typically bound with narrow satin ribbon. Proportions became so exaggerated that samplers were sometimes as long as 3 m (10 ft), while only 10 cm (4 in) wide: the most spectacular example of all is a sampler

A small section of the 'Dowell-Simpson' sampler, a patchwork of different canvasses decorated with Berlin woolwork forms (*The Lady Simpson*)

organised by Mrs Edward Dowell (died 1896), a Norfolk vicar's wife – this piece (now belonging to a descendant) is 12.5 m (41 ft) long! It was exhibited, in its entirety, at the Textile Resource and Research Center of The Valentine Museum, Richmond, V.A., in 1975.

The 'Dowell-Simpson' sampler has a fascinating story to tell. From about 1848 Mrs Dowell asked family and friends to decorate small pieces

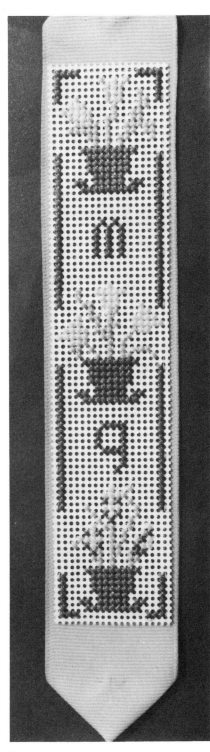

Cross stitches worked on perforated
paper 16×3.3 cm (6¼×1¼ in)

of canvas which she then patiently over the years stitched together. The earlier designs are closely and intricately worked, with most of the canvas covered by stitching. Soon aniline colours, patented by an 18-year-old chemist, William Perkin, in 1856, meant that colours on the sampler became brighter. So, at the same time, did stitches become larger and larger and less of the canvas is covered (you can read all about the sampler and its designs in *The Dowell-Simpson Sampler*, edited by Mildred J. Davis, Textile Resource and Research Center of the Valentine Museum, 1975).

Some Berlin woolwork patterns were used for carpets, stitched with thick woollen cross stitch on wide-meshed canvas. At the 1851 Great Exhibition, Queen Victoria was presented with a 'Ladies' carpet' designed by the architect J.W. Papworth, and stitched in sections by 150 women whose combined efforts, when pieced together, formed a total area of 182 sq. m (1960 sq. ft).

Cross stitch was also used by nineteenth century needleworkers to embellish chair furnishings, standing screens and small pole-screens behind which ladies could protect their complexions. Berlin woolwork died a timely death in the latter half of the nineteenth century, but more subtle patterns continued to be worked, especially on household items.

One unusual form of cross stitch work which might be mentioned here is 'paper embroidery'. Contemporary with Berlin woolwork on canvas, some embroiderers preferred to execute cross and other stitches on card, sometimes called Bristol Board, punched with small round holes set at regular intervals. (Today intrepid needleworkers are once again experimenting with this medium.)

Children's cross stitch sampler working was less prevalent by the end of the century. 'Fine stitching', dressmaking, darning and other mending techniques, with a lot of whitework thrown in for good measure, had taken over as part of a young lady's curriculum.

With the slightly older ladies fine cross stitch continued to be worked as, for instance, monograms on linens. Fabric napkin rings were personalised with cross stitch – the embroidery sometimes worked over a 'waste canvas', especially loose canvas, with every tenth thread blue. (Cross stitch would be worked over canvas and main fabric and then individual threads of the canvas, which had enabled 'counted thread' to be worked on a not-easily-countable fabric, would be withdrawn one by one.)

✿✿✿✿✿✿✿✿✿✿

I should like to mention three twentieth century projects that I consider particularly outstanding.

One is the furnishing of Westwood Manor, Wiltshire (now the property of the National Trust) by Edgar Graham Lister (1873–1956). When he retired from the Foreign Office in 1919 Mr Lister started 'stitching for his house'. There can still be seen the many rice-stitched and other embellished pieces that were used as wall hangings, chair and

43

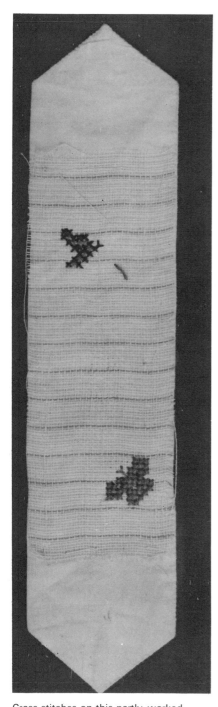

Cross stitches on this partly-worked nineteenth century fabric napkin holder were being executed over the threads of 'waste canvas'. The overall measurements are 19×4.3 cm ($7\frac{1}{2} \times 1\frac{1}{2}$ in). (*Mrs Richard Van Wagenen*)

Chair upholstered with criss-cross corners cross stitching worked by Mr E.G. Lister. (*The National Trust and Mr Denys Sutton*)

A view of Wells Cathedral Choir with some of the superb hangings designed by Lady Hylton during the second quarter of the twentieth century. *(The Dean and Chapter of Wells Cathedral)*

other seat coverings and so on, all worked by Mr Lister.

Not far away from Westwood is Wells Cathedral, parts of which date back to the middle of the thirteenth century. In 1933 the Friends of Wells Cathedral were established to help furnish and look after the cathedral's fabrics. One of their most important undertakings has been the supply of marvellous banner hangings and seat cushions in the choir. Many of the pieces, each unique and designed by Lady Hylton (1874–1962) and subsequently stitched, from 1937 to the early 1950s, by a team of men and women from all over Britain, include cross stitch in the large variety of techniques employed.

There are thirty-nine stall banners commemorating holders of the See of Bath and Wells from 1309 to 1937. There is a stupendous triptych above the Bishop's throne. There are countless chair back and seat and bench cushions, and each embodies intricate symbols. The Wells Cathedral canvasworks are justly famous the world over, and demand a visit if it is at all possible. In America there are many outstanding church needlework projects, in some of which cross stitch, as well as the more popular tent stitch, is employed.

Thus the history of cross stitch reaches our time. And now I shall go travelling once again, all around our world.

3 Around the world with cross stitch

I am lucky enough to have travelled the world many times, and I hope to carry on doing so. Recently, indeed, I was in Hong Kong and there, waiting for the famous 'Star ferry' from Hong Kong Island to Kowloon, on the mainland, was a Chinese woman leading one child by the hand and holding another on her back. The latter baby was in a shoulder papoose made of brightly-coloured red floral cotton fabric with a white applied panel about 25.4 cm (10 in) square which covered the child's back. This panel had red cross stitch motifs which included the 'long life' device illustrated overleaf.

International embroidery surveys have been done before. You may indeed already know my own international books:

> *A World of Embroidery*, Mills & Boon and Scribner's, 1975.
>
> *Embroidery: Traditional Designs, Techniques and Patterns from All Over the World*, Marshall Cavendish Editions, 1977 (published in America as *The Complete International Book of Embroidery*, Simon & Schuster, 1977).

I sketched this Chinese woman in Hong Kong recently; her baby is held in a cross-stitched back carrier

Left
Birds from (a) the Cyclades (b) Peru (c) Corfu and (d) the Ionian Islands.

Cyclades:	7	yellow
	○	blue
	●	black
Peru:	6	blue
	·	yellow
Corfu:	~	red
Ionia:	○	black
	/	green
	r	red
	·	yellow

Rather then be *complete*, in this instance, I thought I would set down a few personal observations of places and designs.

It is possible to categorise cross stitch of the world in so many different ways. Here I have illustrated more or less *thematically* so that you can have a better choice of motif. By contrast, I have purposely written the text as a conversational summary with ideas for further reading and study.

You will notice that much of the decoration I mention is on garments, especially women's blouses and dresses. If you are particularly interested in dressmaking and would like to try making up your own cross-stitched designs, I would suggest that you might find helpful ideas in the book by Dorothy K. Burnham, *Cut my Cote*, Royal Ontario Museum, 1973.

You will probably *not* want, I should think, to emulate the embroidered 'baggy pants' from the northern hill tribes area of Thailand, one of the few exciting regions *south* of the Equator where cross stitch is still being worked. Centred around Chiang Mai are such itinerant tribes

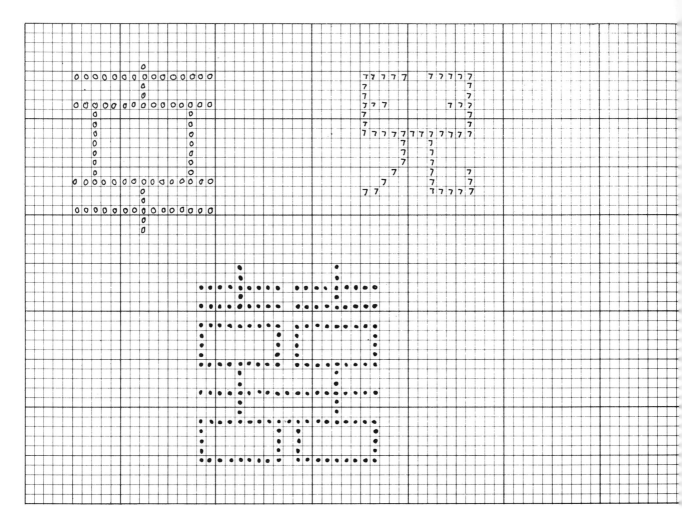

as the Yao, Meo and others who have traditional stitcheries. It is the women of the Yao and Meo who most concern us from a cross stitch point of view, however. They learn as early as the age of four how to stitch; it is said that men determine whether or not an (older) girl would make a suitable bride by her embroidery, particularly that on the legs of her baggy trousers!

I am fortunate enough to have a pair of Yao trousers. The fullness of the main body of the garment, made of black linen, is gathered to a dark blue waistband 10 cm (4 in) wide. From 8 cm (3 in) below this waistband right to the bottom of the mid-calf, tight and cuffless hems there is a panel of stitching, 63 cm (24 in) high, 44 cm (17 in) wide, worked in back and stem stitches, pattern darning – and cross stitch.

Generally only five colours of embroidery thread are used; red, yellow, dark green, dark blue and white. It is suggested that perhaps this 'colour quintet' is related to Ben Jarong (five colour) porcelain, introduced from China in the nineteenth century. Although sometimes commercial

Hong Kong:
Among the motifs on the baby carrier is the longevity motif (at bottom)

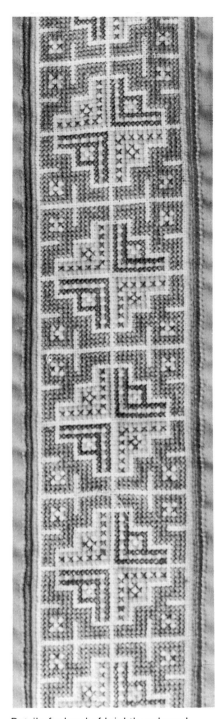

Detail of a band of brightly-coloured cross stitching from the northern hill tribes of Thailand. The piece, bound with shocking pink nylon ribbon, is 5 cm (2 in) wide

threads are used today in place of locally-dyed silk threads, adherence to a maximum of six colours is generally respected.

Yao cross stitch is of uniform size, with about 32 cross stitches per 5 centimetres (16 per inch), over two warp and weft threads of fabric. Over 100 geometric patterns are in use, and in each case it is colour contrast rather than design contour which is dominant. As well as trousers, Yao women decorate their children's hats, horse cruppers, the last 45 cm (18 in) or so of their own sashes and turbans, special New Year aprons and the lower right hand corners of the fronts of their husbands' jackets.

Chaing Mai is an hour's flight from Bangkok and there are many tours and excursions. You can go to see Yao and Meo stitching for yourself. If you are pressed for time, however, you can also now find excellent examples of both tribes' work in shops in the capital. Right in the centre of Bangkok, five minutes' walk from Jim Thompson's house (he who is credited with the inspiration for those marvellous brightly-coloured Thai silks) is the Thai Hill-Crafts Foundation in Srapatum Palace. It is well worth a visit. And if you want to read more about Yao and Meo work I suggest:

> Jacqueline Butler, *Yao Design*, Siam Society, 1970
>
> Margaret Campbell, *From the Hands of the Hills*, J. S. Uberoi, Hong Kong, 1978.

From one country from which I have just once again returned to an area I know well and dearly love. . . .

I first developed my fascination with cross stitch when living and working in the Middle East. I was helping a group of American women to catalogue, under the auspices of the United Nations Relief and Welfare Association, traditional Palestinian needlework motifs. We designed summer handbags, pocketbooks and cushion covers using some of the designs that had for many generations customarily been worked by women on their own clothing.

The intent was to keep alive traditional motifs, many of them symbolic and most of them charmingly named. I remember, for instance, 'chickens' feet' – no need to describe that one – and 'road to Egypt' (a particularly twisting design) and 'old man's teeth' (rather uneven, to say the least).

Levantine cross stitching is generally a distaff skill, worked on women's clothing, primarily on front yoke panels (*kabbas*), sleeves and vertically covering seams of long-sleeved full length dresses and open robes. Materials and designs vary considerably from region to region.

One of the best surveys of cross stitching in this area was undertaken by Phyllis Sutton and Grace Crowfoot in the 1930s. Mrs Sutton's husband was a missionary in Ramallah, a Christian town near Jerusalem, and the two ladies were able to study a community especially famed for their stitching.

Ramallah girls learnt their skills at an early age, for it was customary to

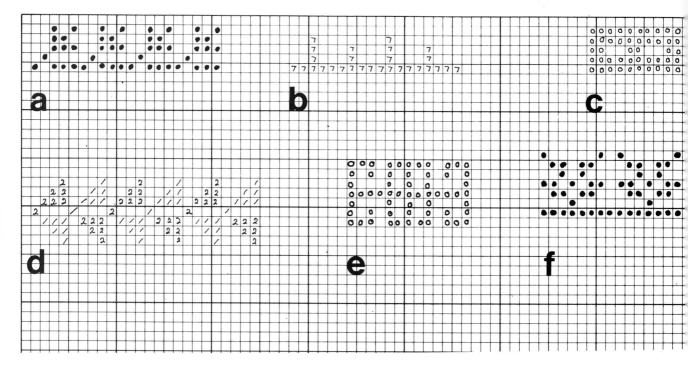

have as many as 13 embroidered gowns in their trousseaux. Fortunately for some of the younger and less adept brides, however, stitching was not only itself a communal and social effort, with women sitting together to talk and stitch, but tradition included the handing down of one gown to many owners. Some robes, indeed, can be seen to have been let out and/or taken in, depending on the girth of the current wearer. Such sociable stitching did not lessen concentration: if a Ramallah worker failed to cross a stitch it was suggested that she had 'fallen into the sin of sloth'.

Unlike most Middle Eastern costume styles, which are black or dark blue, the Ramallah dress can be identified by its natural linen colouring. Its long sleeves are winged and the main embroidery was in the past executed in red and black silk from Damascus, though later examples display commercial stranded cottons, sometimes with green added to the colouring.

Several excellent collections of Ramallah and other Middle Eastern cross stitched gowns are now well displayed. You may have a chance to visit the Museum of Popular Folk Art and Traditions next to the Philadelphia Hotel in Amman, Jordan. You may already know the Museum of Mankind in London. I would also suggest the Royal Ontario Museum in Toronto. As far as further reading is concerned you should look out for:

Shelagh Weir, *The Traditional Costumes of the Arab Women of Palestine*, British Museum, 1970.

Palestinian embroidery patterns include (a) chickens' feet (b) old man's teeth (c) bachelor's cushion (d) old man upside down (e) road to Egypt and (f) flower pot motifs. You can use any colours

Hilary Wharton wears a full-length, open gown from the Galilee area

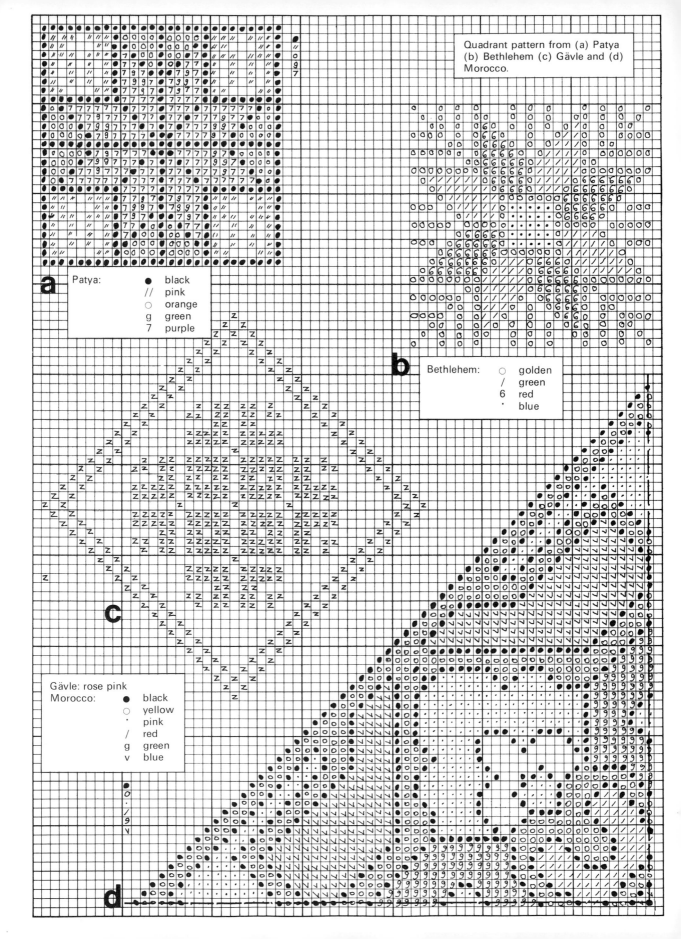

Quadrant pattern from (a) Patya
(b) Bethlehem (c) Gävle and (d)
Morocco.

a Patya:
● black
// pink
○ orange
g green
7 purple

b Bethlehem:
○ golden
/ green
6 red
· blue

c

Gävle: rose pink
Morocco:
● black
○ yellow
· pink
/ red
g green
v blue

d

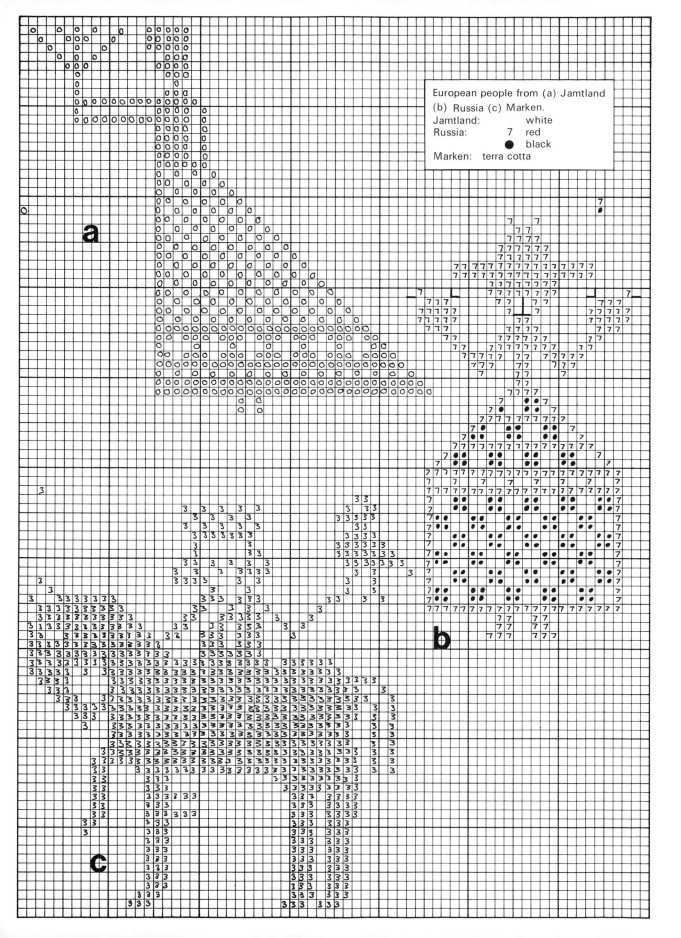

European people from (a) Jamtland
(b) Russia (c) Marken.
Jamtland: white
Russia: 7 red
● black
Marken: terra cotta

Another marvellous museum from a cross stitch – and many other – point of view is the Museum of Anthropology in Mexico City. I was taken there recently by two charming Mexican ladies who had been to a morning lecture I gave on 'Needlework travels', Maria Luisa Santacruz and Margarita Reyes. We were to go to the museum and on to La Fonda del Recuerdo for a typical 2.30 p.m. Mexican lunch.

I was in for two REAL treats (yes, lunch afterwards was also absolutely memorable). The museum is a TREASURE HOUSE of cross stitch. The whole of the upper floor of this spacious U-shaped modern construction is devoted to displays of various Mexican lifestyles. There is a Nayarit scene, from north-west of Mexico City, which includes a priest wearing an outfit liberally embroidered with cross stitch reindeer motifs. From the south of the country, a Chiapas man (of whom there are, thanks to intermarriage, now only about three thousand left) wears a *huipil*, shirt, with a cross-stitched yoke.

One of the most colourful of all the costumes is that worn by a model in the Santa Catarina display, from the centre of the Huichol highlands. Many parts of the costume are cross-stitched; women decorate their menfolk's *rahuareros*, long overshirts and *shavereshs*, mid-calf trousers, with similar patterns. They also decorate and form unusual *cosihuires* or *queitzaruames*, waist belts formed of little cross-stitched bags, hanging side by side and joined at their tops, the two lower corners of each bag embellished with tassels the same colour red as the cross stitching.

I was so excited, indeed, by that belt that after I got back to England I made my own Mexican belt-bag – and you too can make one (see p. 108).

One of the best-known regions of the world for cross stitch is Scandinavia, and much of the best-known cross stitching comes from the Svealand area north of Stockholm. Once the area was noted for intensive flax cultivation, which meant that cross stitch was worked on locally-produced linen fabrics. Imported and expensive cotton fabrics were later much prized.

Swedish women traditionally decorated household items, especially table linens, as well as collars, cuffs and other clothing pieces. They stitched geometric designs but, unlike the Thai and Middle Eastern embroiderers already mentioned, they also used motifs recognisable as, say, hearts and wheels and stars.

Perhaps three particular Swedish styles are pre-eminent in any study of the country's cross stitching today. One is *Delsbo work*, found especially in north-east Svealand, in the Hudiksvall area. This is recognised by blue and red star and heart-shaped motifs on natural or white linen. Another is *Järvsö work*, also from the same area, characterised by rose-coloured star and other motifs, sometimes with attached thread tassels.

The third recognisable style is *Svartstickläna*, 'Swedish blackwork', from the Darlana region, identified by minute black silk cross stitches forming dense diamond blocks and other geometric formations, often with one motif repeated several times. A woman's shawl, a *tupphalskädena*, made from about 60 cm (24 in) square of fine linen or cotton,

Huichol man, from Santa Catarina, sketched in the Museum of Anthropology, Mexico City. Cross stitch embellishes his tunic and trousers and the 'bag-belt', which inspired me later to design the project shown on p. 108

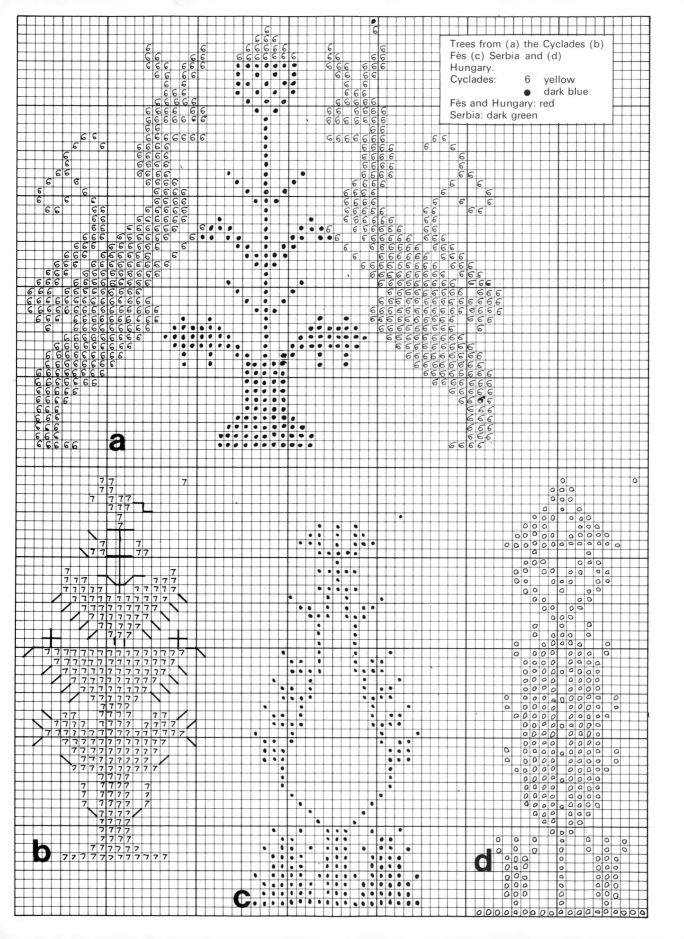

Trees from (a) the Cyclades (b)
Fès (c) Serbia and (d)
Hungary.
Cyclades: 6   yellow
            ●   dark blue
Fès and Hungary: red
Serbia: dark green

a

b

c

d

might have three adjacent diamond motifs in three corners of the cloth, the points connected by narrow zigzag bands. As well as cross stitch, satin stitch and pattern darning might be used, and hanging tassels might embellish the corners. (You can read all about a particularly beautiful 1809 shawl in *Counted Thread*, the magazine of the Counted Thread Society, March 1981, 3.)

No mention of Scandinavian cross stitch would be complete without due obeisance to 'Danish work', fostered so magnificently by the Danish Handcraft Guild that cross stitch is known in some parts of the world as 'Danish cross stitch'.

The Guild was founded in 1928 to revive traditional designs, and such ladies as Gerda Bengtsson and Gertie Wandel indeed deserve laurel wreaths for their design – and their dedication. Since 1940, indeed, Gerda Bengtsson, an artist trained at the Danish Academy of Arts, has developed a recognisable transposition of marvellously realistic flowers and other graceful motifs into cross stitch.

If you would like to see some more Scandiniavian designs, I recommend making contact with one of the Danish Handcraft Guild addresses list given at the back of this book.

✩✩✩✩✩✩✩✩✩✩

You will notice that many of the line drawings displayed thematically here are taken from countries now wholly or partly within the Soviet Union – Armenia, Estonia, Belorussia and the Ukraine, for instance – and elsewhere in east and south-east Europe. Here women work cross stitches, mostly on white or natural linen, for their own and others' clothing and for household items.

Perhaps most characteristic of costume embellishment of a particular region is the woman's blouse. There are three distinct cuts. A basic design from Romania and parts of the Ukraine has the main body and long gathered-cuff raglan sleeves gathered at the neck. There may be dense cross stitching across both shoulders and in narrow strips along the sleeves and from neck to hem of the front and back of the main body. Another gathered-neckline blouse, found in Turkey, Greece and the Aegean Islands, has extra fabric inset as body sides extending to underarms, and sleeves are gathered a few inches above their full extension to form a same-fabric gathered cuff. Embroidery is generally found in blocks from the shoulders down the upper sleeves and as gathered cuff and front yoke decoration.

The last of the 'blouse trio' has no gathers. Sleeves are set into the body as are men's shirt sleeves and the neck opening is simply a circular hole with front vertical slit. The main embroidery embellishment on this type of blouse, found in Ukraine and in Macedonia and elsewhere where Turkish influence has been felt, is in solid blocks on the upper sleeves, from a few centimetres below the shoulder seam right down to the open hem. and in blocks bordering the front neck slit and perhaps as vertical bands on the main body. If this style is extended to form a full length dress, decoration is also found solidly worked around the main hem.

One of the densely-packed diagram sheets in the Ukranian Women's Association of Canada's Bucovinian folio

For that really professional *touch, remember – when making up a cross-stitch piece – carefully to* press *it at each stage of construction*

I have recently been introduced to a large folio, *Ukrainian Bucovinian Cross-stitch Embroidery* (Eastern Executive of the Ukrainian Women's Association of Canada, 1974) which contains 74 large sheets densely-packed with colour graphs of typical motifs from Bucovina, the eastern European territory containing part of the north-east Carpathian Mountains, divided after 1947 between Romania and the Soviet Union. I have seldom seen a more detailed study of needlework of an area. The accompanying text, in Ukrainian, English and French, is a translation of notes by Eric Kolbenhier and it goes into the minutiae of the socio-historical background to Bucovinian embroidery. The red and black graphs are superb; many of the patterns would look lovely as border embellishment on clothing.

Red is, indeed, the most popular colour in many of the cross stitches from east and south-east Europe. In the Silesian area of Poland motifs, unworked, are surrounded by worked reserves, in 'Assisi' style. In Hungary, upright cross stitches are sometimes worked on a trellis of laid threads. Red cross stitch motifs in Bulgaria are often outlined in lines of black back stitches which sometimes extend beyond the periphery of the enclosed motif to form little tangent 'hooks'.

It is mainly *motifs* that indicate the origin of a particular piece of work. 'Earth mother' or 'baba' shapes often come from within the Soviet Union. Stars are often associated with northern regions. The 'tree of life', however stylised, is found in many areas with past Turkish influence. A peacock motif from the Ionian islands is much plumper than his counterpart from Corfu. Interlinked squares and other geometric shapes are often found in cross stitching from the Cyclades.

Not surprisingly, in view of trade and religious trends, many of the cross stitch ideas from the north-east Mediterranean have been carried to north-west Africa, particularly Algeria and Morocco. In Algeria, 'double herringbone', with two differently-coloured threads worked one and then another to produce a line of alternately-coloured stitches, is found, In Morocco the ordinary form of cross stitch is preferred by some, though there are local variants. In Azemmour, for instance, a form of 'Assisi work' is characterised by peacocks with exaggeratedly long tails. In Casablanca there are cross-stitched tree motifs with feathery branches. In Salé, monochrome work, often in salmon-coloured silk, is popular, and motifs may include especially tall and fountain-like versions of the 'tree of life'. In the Fès area, cross stitch is recognisable for carefully-planned symmetrical corner 'fillers' with stylised flowers and candelabra shapes.

✩✩✩✩✩✩✩✩✩✩

This has been far from a complete treatise on all aspects of cross stitching all round the world. But perhaps it has given you some inkling of the many types of cross stitch that you can come across as you travel, perhaps on business, perhaps on vacation.

I hope this conversational exposure has given you *ideas for your own stitching*. Yes, it is time for ideas. And it is time to talk about *designing for yourself*. . . .

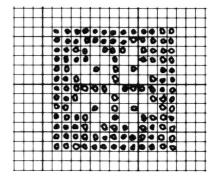

Silesian motif worked in 'Assisi' style

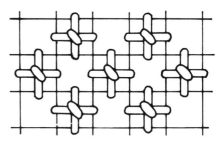

Hungarian cross stitch on a laid trellis

Double herringbone, Algerian style

Right
Eastern European flowers from (a) the Caucasus (b) and (c) the Ukraine (d) Slovakia and (e) Russia.

Caucasus:	●	green
	7	yellow
	○	dark red
	·	lighter red
	p	purple
	=	orange
Ukraine:	g	green
	/	pink
	=	orange
	○	purple
	●	black
	⫫	red
Slovakia:	7	red
	●	black
Russia:	●	black
	/	red
	s	green
	○	blue

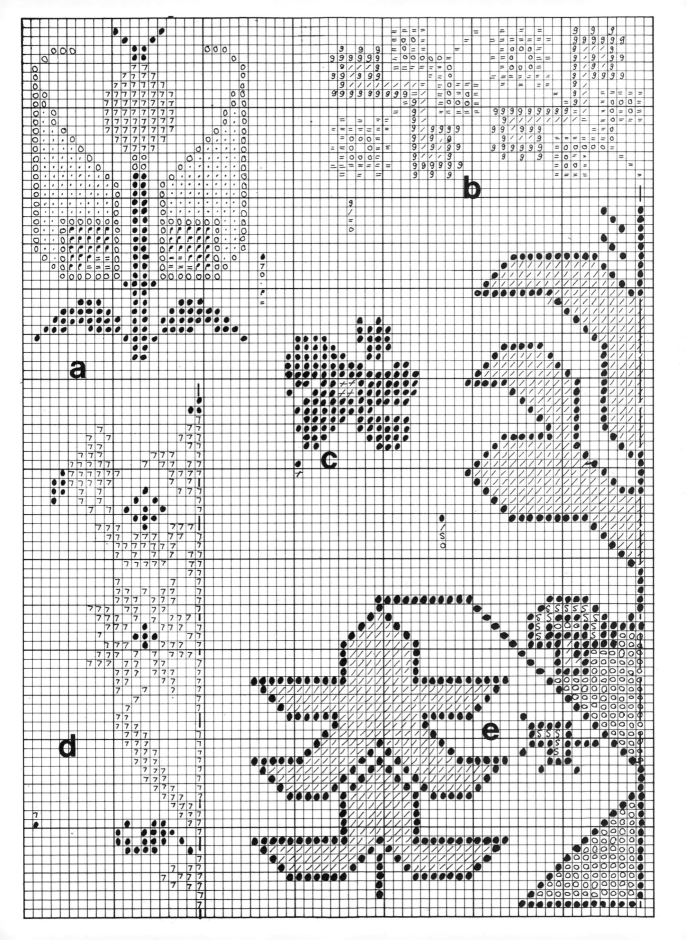

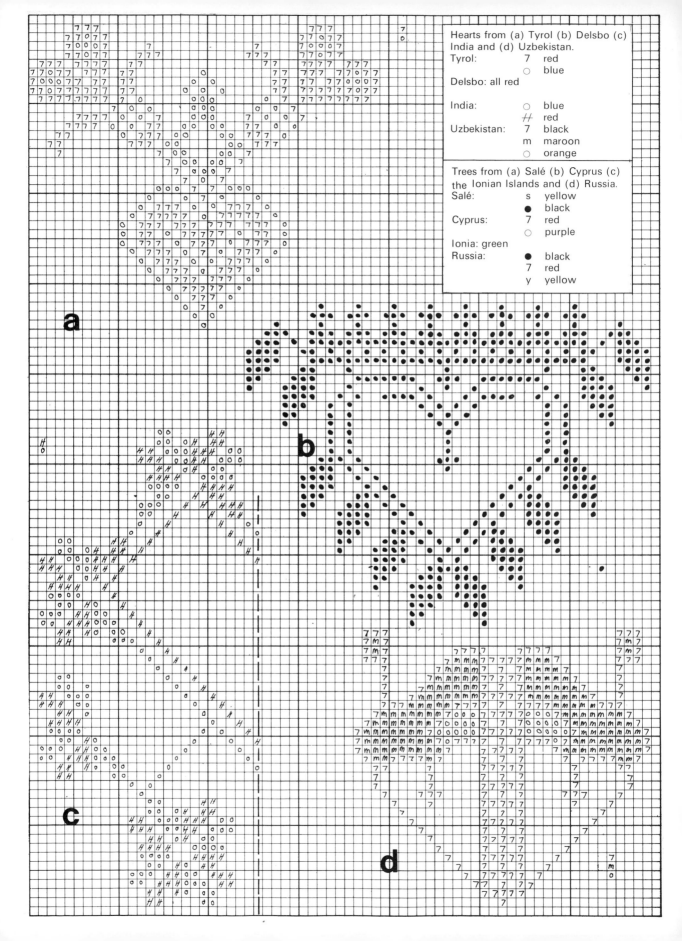

Hearts from (a) Tyrol (b) Delsbo (c)
India and (d) Uzbekistan.

Tyrol: 7 red
○ blue

Delsbo: all red

India: ○ blue
red

Uzbekistan: 7 black
m maroon
○ orange

Trees from (a) Salé (b) Cyprus (c)
the Ionian Islands and (d) Russia.

Salé: s yellow
● black

Cyprus: 7 red
○ purple

Ionia: green

Russia: ● black
7 red
y yellow

a

b

c

d

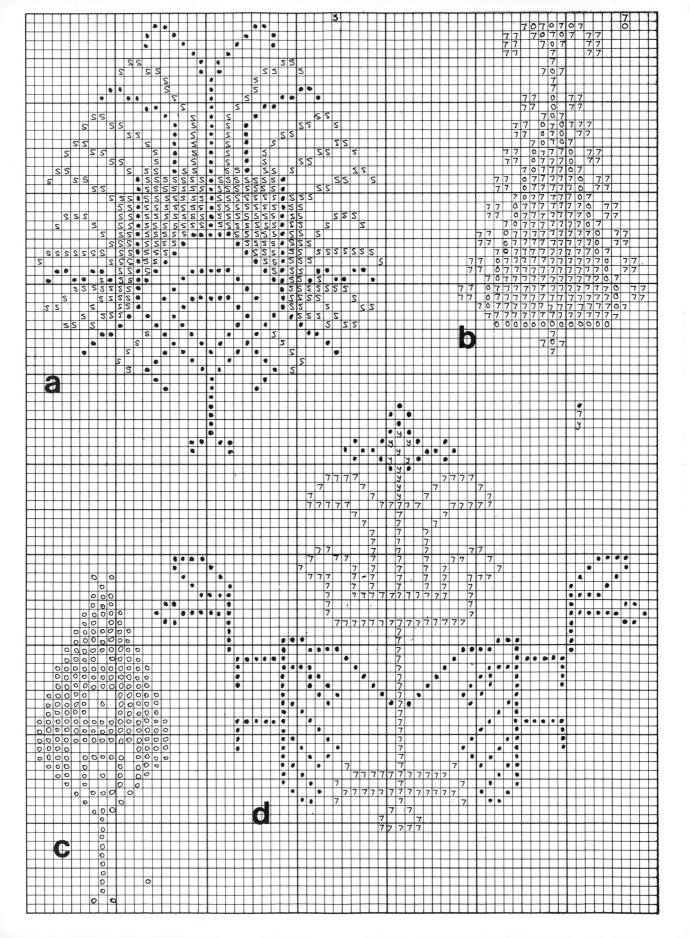

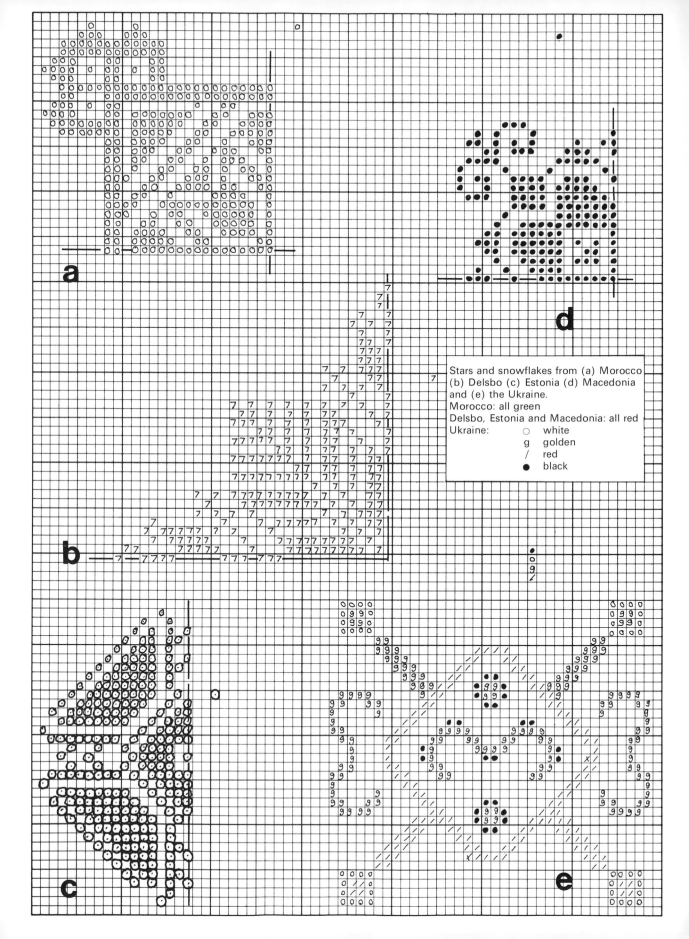

Stars and snowflakes from (a) Morocco
(b) Delsbo (c) Estonia (d) Macedonia
and (e) the Ukraine.
Morocco: all green
Delsbo, Estonia and Macedonia: all red
Ukraine: ○   white
            g   golden
            /   red
            ●   black

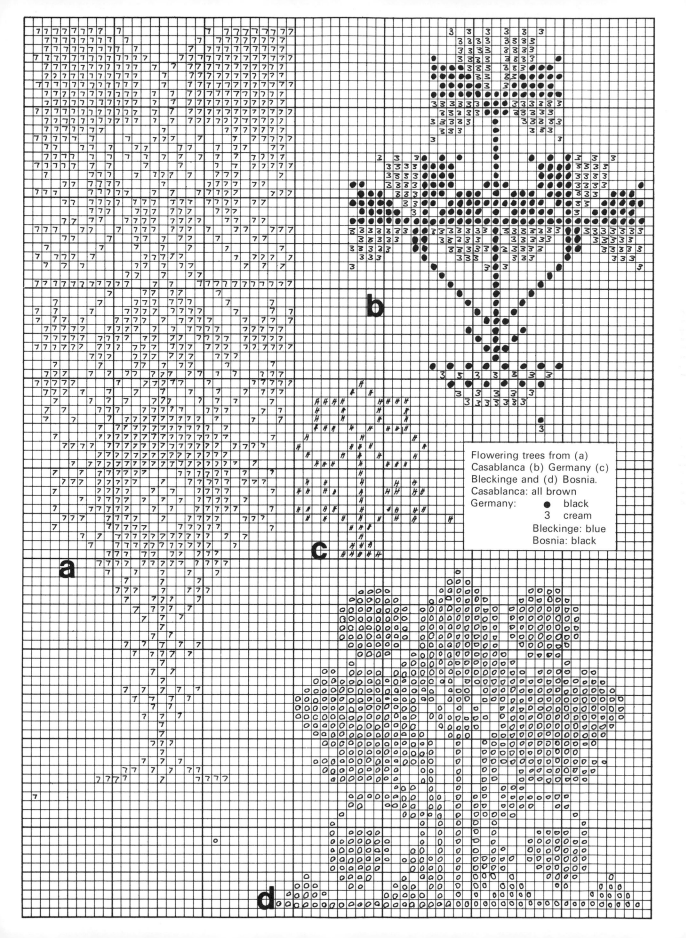

Flowering trees from (a)
Casablanca (b) Germany (c)
Bleckinge and (d) Bosnia.
Casablanca: all brown
Germany: ● black
3 cream
Bleckinge: blue
Bosnia: black

a

b

c

d

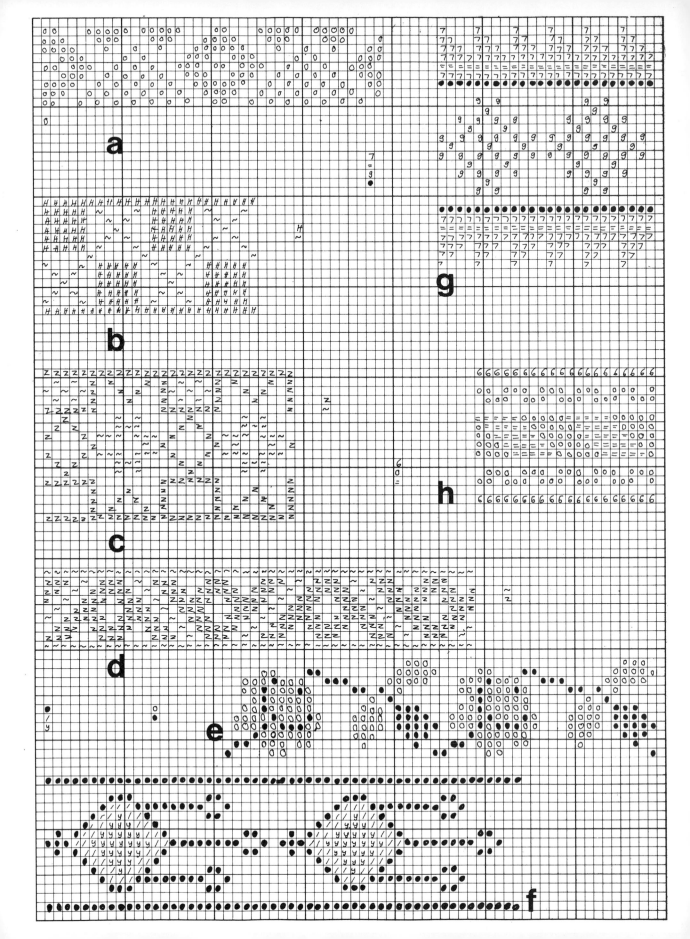

4 Designs for cross stitch

Graphed or charted motifs are offered in profusion throughout this book – and if you do not know how to transpose them as cross stitch on fabric you can find instructions for graph-following on p. 18.

You may want to know, however, how to 'site' motifs. You may want to know whether or not a particular motif will fit on to the area of fabric available (nothing is more frustrating than nearly to finish a design only to find that there simply is not enough room for those last few crosses!). You may also want a few tips on thinking of, and preparing, your *own* designs for cross stitch. . . .

I should like to suggest, first of all, that you start keeping *your own design file*. In this you can keep cuttings, your own drawings, photographs, colour swatches that you like – things to *inspire* and things to *remind* you.

I was myself tremendously inspired recently when I was shown, by Thelma Nye, a transcription and notes by Eileen O'Connor, of a folio, published in Germany in 1879, of records and illustrations of cross stitch patterns compiled by Professor Julius Lessing. His careful graphing of patterns has resulted in a whole wealth of design ideas.

And so, I hope, will *your* design file and notes similarly inspire you.

An ordinary A4 ring binder with clear plastic pocket leaves formed from suitably-sized strong plastic bags – with holes punched with an office hole puncher – makes an excellent design file. Drawings, samples and 'ideas' photographs stored in the pockets can easily be seen. They can swiftly be taken out of the pockets when required.

☆☆☆☆☆☆☆☆☆

Alternatively, why not *make yourself a design binder*?

My cross-stitched file contains photographic 'pages' formed of the clear plastic containers I have already mentioned. The binder is held together with a twisted cord formed of the same coloured stranded cottons as were used for the decoration of the front of the binder. The covers are pale blue and the front is embellished with a repeating sweet pea design worked in two shades of purple, pale pink and bright green.

Left

Border designs from all around: (a) and (f) Uzbekistan (b,c,d) Netherlands (e) Ukraine (g) the Yao and (h) India.

Uzbek:	○	red
	y	yellow
	●	black
	/	blue
Netherlands:	#	mustard
	~	orange
	z	dark green
Ukraine:	○	red
	●	black
Yao:	7	red
	=	yellow
	●	black
	g	green
Indian:	6	blue
	○	red
	=	yellow

To Make Your Own 30 × 24 cm (12¼ × 9½ in) Binder You Will Need:

40 cm (16 in) pale blue Aida, 6 blocks per centimetre (15 blocks per inch)

Area felt (I used dark green but you might prefer blue to match the Aida) 30 × 48 cm (12 × 19 in)

4 pieces of strong card, two 30 × 21 cm (12 × 8 in), two 30 × 4 cm (12 × 1½ in)

1 skein each all-purpose sewing thread (pale blue) and DMC 894 (pink), 550 (dark purple), 553 (pale purple), 906 (green)

Tapestry 24 needle.

Cut two Aida shapes 40 × 30 cm (16 × 12 in). Tack an area 30 × 21 cm (12 × 8 in) to one side of one of the shapes. Now, starting at A, stitch the design, working in *two strands*, with cross stitches over *1 block* of fabric.

Only one 'repeat' of the pattern is given. Work repeats of the pattern right to the tacked lines.

When you have finished stitching, remove your tackings, Turn the fabric wrong side up and place one large and one small card shape so that the large shape covers the cross-stitched area of fabric and the smaller one is parallel to it, 1.5 cm (⅝ in) away from it.

Carefully glue (or *lace*, if you have an aversion to glue) the surplus fabric in place. Do not use too much adhesive. I glue by first spreading a *minute* amount of adhesive on the card and then placing the card on the appropriate part of the fabric. Then I fold the corners of the surplus fabric over, diagonal to the edges of the card, and finally I fold over the main surplus.

This will be the front of your file: prepare the other (back) shape in the same manner but with no cross stitch embellishment.

Now glue appropriate shapes of felt on to both shapes. Using your fine-pointed embroidery scissors as a stiletto, make two holes, 9 cm (3½ in) apart, equidistant from the centre, in what will be the 'hinge' between the two cards on each of your two shapes. Bind the circumference of the holes with overstitching or button hole stitching in pale blue thread.

Use left-over pink and dark purple stranded cottons to make a twisted cord. Place your plastic pockets, holes punched, between the shapes, and hold the 'sandwich' with your twisted cord threaded through the holes.

Note: you might like to spray both front and back with Scotchgard fabric protector to prevent dirt.

✩✩✩✩✩✩✩✩✩

Now you have your binder all ready you can *start storing ideas*. All good professional designers have a sketch-and-ideas file. I am now going to suggest one or two little exercises that you can store in your file . . . so make sure you have pencils, paper and graph and clear tracing paper to hand.

You will need two Aida shapes for the binder, broken lines denote subsequent placing of larger and smaller pieces of card

Having difficulty remembering in which direction your 'upper diagonal' should face? Refer constantly to the 'symbolic key' temporarily stitched in an upper corner of your fabric

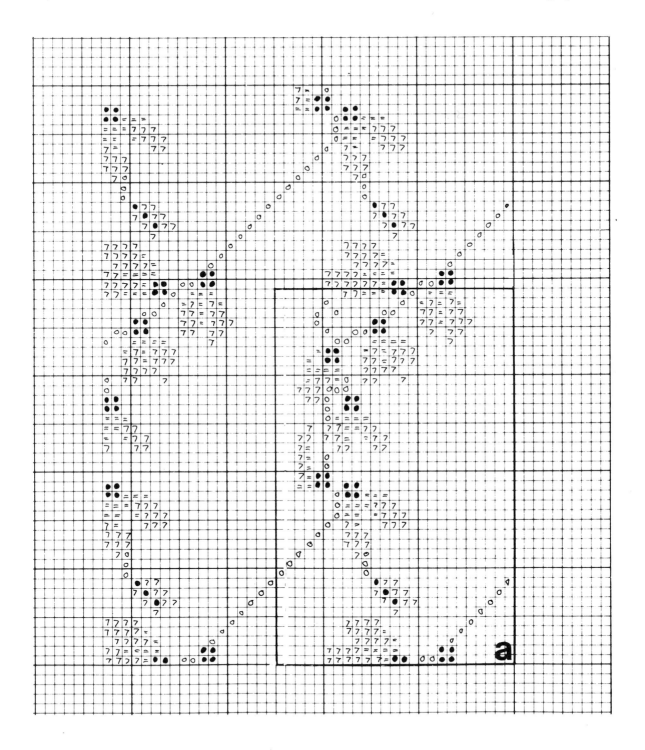

A simple motif (here boxed) is repeated
over all the fabric that will cover a larger
card

○   green
=   pale purple
●   dark purple
7   pink

Balance – and How to 'Site' Your Motifs

Regardless of whether or not you are following one of my motifs from this book, or whether you are going to create your own design, it is important to end up with a work that looks balanced. This is not to say that it must be symmetrical. If I am designing, say, a sampler I do not necessarily have identical lion 'supporters', one either side of a central coat of arms. I might have a lion supporter one side and unicorn on the other but the unicorn would occupy the *same total area* of fabric as the lion.

If you are planning a design with several different motifs on it it really does help to 'graph out' the whole thing first. Divide your graph paper into quadrants before you sketch.

Sketch, using your pencil *as lightly as possible*. Make sure that your design is balanced from one side to the other of the central marking. As far as vertical balance is concerned it is better to err towards bottom-heavy. You might find that you want more of your pattern below the central dividing line rather than above it.

Try sketching a few doodle-layouts. Divide rectangles on a piece of plain paper into quadrants and roughly sketch in motifs with a concentration of density at the top and another with density at the bottom. Don't you agree that the bottom-heavy looks the better of the two?

Are you stuck for *doodle ideas*?

Take a copy of *Good Housekeeping*, *Family Circle* or another general 'women's magazine' and sketch out some of the commodities shown in advertisements . . . a stick of butter, cup and saucer, a cow, tube of toothpaste . . . unrelated motifs. But sketch them, and try 'balancing' one motif with another in marked quadrants on your sketching paper. Alternatively, borrow a children's farmyard or fairy story book and sketch out motifs that are related . . . all farmyard animals, for instance . . . and similarly try balancing them on your drawing sheet.

How Do You Work Out Whether Your Design Will Fit into a Linen Space?

I find that a calculator and a ruler are the best method of making sure that a motif or complete design does not extend beyond the required area of my linen. This is the procedure to follow:

1 How many graph squares to the inch? (say 10).
2 How many stitches to the inch? (say $14\frac{1}{2}$ if I am working over 2 threads of linen with 29 threads per inch).
3 My motif measures 33 cm (13 in) high on the graph paper
4 therefore I calculate 13 × 10 ÷ 14.5 to find that
5 the motif will occupy a fraction under 23 cm (9 in) of linen.

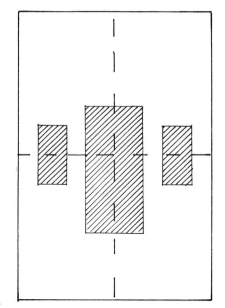
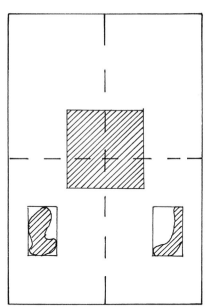

Symmetry of design. If motifs either side of the central line are not exactly equal, they should occupy a similar total area (lower drawing). Greater density should appear in the lower rather than upper half of a design

I do find it invaluable *always to compute before stitching*. I am an experienced 'eyeballer', practised at judging whether or not something will fit. But even I know I cannot exactly trust my own judgement.

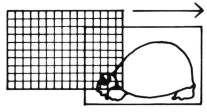

Graphed tracing paper can be placed above an illustration and the design traced through

Holyroodhouse (outlined in dark blue back stitch)
- ○   mustard
- 7   scarlet
- y   yellow
- =   pale blue
- ●   dark blue
- ⊙   dark blue cross stitches should be worked over all this area

How to Prepare a Graph Design Or Motif

All praise and thanks to the inventor of graph tracing paper . . , without it designing specifically for cross stitch must have been a nightmare!

However today it is, fortunately, almost like a dream . . .

All you do is simply lay your graph tracing paper over a photograph, line drawing, painting – and trace your design through, *blocking off whole squares* rather than producing a fluid line going through a square.

Could anything be easier?

You notice that I say 'block off whole squares'. I should mention that some people prefer to design by marking the lines at the edges of squares. These marked lines indicate the periphery of an area of the pattern. My own preferred method is to mark *squares* (equalling subsequent *stitches*) and leave line markings to indicate highlighting of a design. You can see what I mean by looking at the drawing of Holyroodhouse here: each marked square equals a stitch and marked lines are embellishing backstitches worked later as highlights to the design.

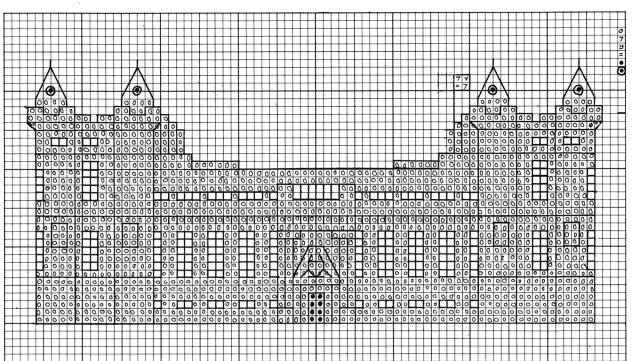

How to Graph Your Own House

Yes, you can graph your house or another building of your choice!

You use the same method as that outlined above. You will need a suitably-sized photograph or drawing (if your illustration is the wrong size, look at the directions for size-changing below). How do you know if your illustration IS the right size? Work out the space-calculation at the beginning of this chapter, working the calculations 'in reverse', that is to say:

1 How high is the area of linen you want your 'house' to occupy? (say 25 cm, 10 in).

2 How many squares per inch of your graph paper? (say 10).

3 How many stitches per inch of linen? (say $14\frac{1}{2}$ if you are working over 2 threads of linen with 29 threads per inch).

4 Therefore you would calculate $10 \times 14.5 \div 10$ to find that

5 You need an illustration with the building 37 cm ($14\frac{1}{2}$ in) high from which to trace a graphed motif that will occupy 25 cm (10 in) height of linen.

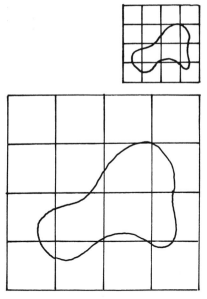

If your illustration is the wrong size you can *enlarge or reduce it*. There are two ways of doing this:

1 Trace your drawing on to graph tracing paper with *more* squares per inch (if your illustration is too small) or on to graph tracing paper with *fewer* squares per inch (if your illustration is too large). Then, if you feel happier when counting from your 'usual' graph paper, you can count squares from the one, marked, graph paper on to your usual graph paper. Alternatively, you can stitch directly from the marked graph paper.

2 Make an enlarged or reduced drawing from your wrong-sized illustration. I do this by the following method. I lay a piece of plain tracing paper over the wrong-sized photograph and mark the area of tracing paper covering the photograph into quadrants, and each quarter into quadrants again so that I have 16 squares in all. I take a piece of paper marked with and area the size I want my illustration and similarly divide this area into 16. Then I copy, one square after another, so that the illustration is reproduced as the correct size on the right-sized piece of paper.

Enlarging or reducing a design

How to Prepare Curves and Circles

So easy – when you know how!

To prepare a curve, first either pencil your curve as a fluid line on to graph paper or place graph tracing paper over the curve drawn on another sheet of (ordinary) paper. Then, with your pencil, block off whole squares on the graph paper as neatly as possible following the line of the curve. When you have finished look at what you have blocked off and see if it

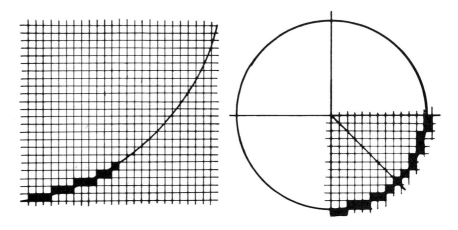

To block off a curve, first draw a fluid line and block accordingly. When

blocking a circle, work one quarter, half of which is a mirror image of the other

looks 'right'. You may have to erase one or two squares or you may have to block off more squares.

Since I always find it easier to *add rather than to subtract* when graphing I tend initially to do too few rather than too many blockings.

To graph a circle, block out one quarter of the circle, as illustrated. You will notice that one half of that quarter (i.e. one-eighth of the whole) should be an exact mirror image of the other half of that quarter.

Colour

Many cross stitch pieces look best worked in monochrome – that is to say, in *one colour*. Traditionally, and ideally, that colour should be strong and easily visible to produce the most striking design impact.

I do recommend that if you are using *more than one colour* you hold those coloured threads together and view them next to the intended fabric. It is annoying if, after you have started stitching, you introduce another colour which, on reflection, simply does not complement the colours you have already worked.

You may find it easier, as I have already indicated, to stitch from a *coloured* graph. If this is so, you will probably colouring your graphs with *symbolic* rather than with actual colours; even with the vast number of felt pens and crayons in my studio I seldom have one the exact shade of the stranded cotton that it is meant to imply. You cannot therefore judge from a graph whether or not colours are complementary. You must actually hold the threads together.

Colour makes such a difference to the finished effect even of a simple block motif. I took a basic four-by-four-square and colour coded it in ten different ways. I describe those colours next to the illustration and graph.

Why not work your own little *colour block sampler*? You could keep it in your design file so that you can constantly be reminded of which colours you like with which.

Left-handed? Place the book in front of a mirror to be able to follow the stitch diagrams

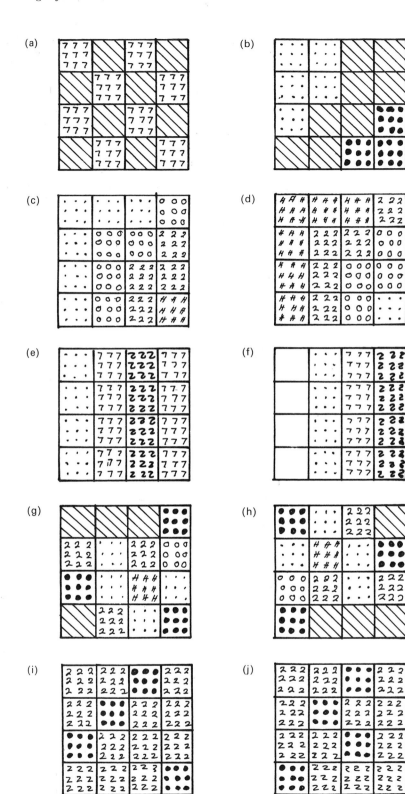

(a)

(b)

(c)

(d)

(e)

(f)

(g)

(h)

(i)

(j)

Colour exercise:
(a) simple chequerboard (b) light to
dark, down to lower right (c) and (d)
exact reversals of colours (e) vertical
stripes (f) vertical stripes, lightest to left
(g) is turned through 180° to produce
(h) and in (i) and (j) a simple horizontal
row is moved one stage to the right or
left.

7	pale blue
\	bright green
·	yellow
●	dark green
○	palest pink
2	medium pink
#	red
2	dark blue

. . . and the colour-coded graph
produces this

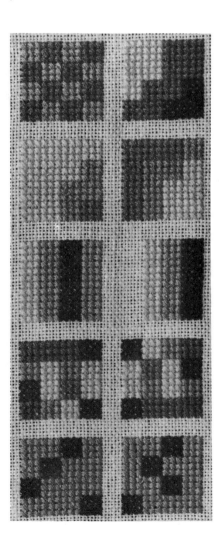

And now for ideas. . . .

The first thing that a designer has to remember is constantly to be *alert* for ideas. Magazines, newspapers, photographs, fabric swatches. If you see any motif or pattern illustrated and you can possibly do so, cut it out – and store it in your design file.

Sometimes of course you cannot 'cut it out' (beauty parlours do not take kindly to magazine-eaters). I know several designers who never go anywhere without their cameras so that they can always record something that has caught their eye.

If you haven't a camera, sketch what you see. It doesn't matter how rough your sketch is; you can perfect it later. Even the roughest sketch will more accurately remind you what something was like than mere memory.

I love to sketch. The three patterns labelled 'Jakarta hotel room', for instance, were all originally jotted down on a telephone memo pad by my bed.

Look for adaptable designs in other needleworks. Transposition from canvas work, another counted thread form, to cross stitch is taken pretty

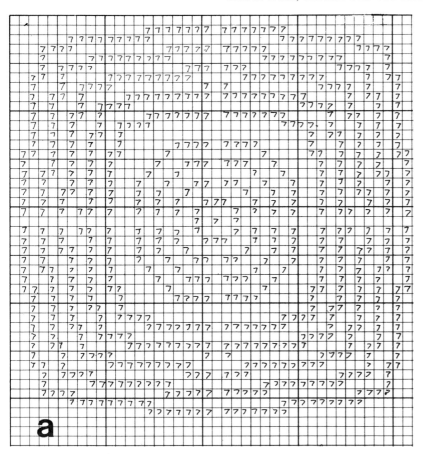

'Jakarta hotel room' – sketches made in my lovely room at the Hotel Borobudur: (a) the hotel's logo (b) design taken from the canework surrounding the wall mirror and (c) (*overleaf*) the decorative iron railing set in brick work that formed my balcony balustrade. Choose your own colours

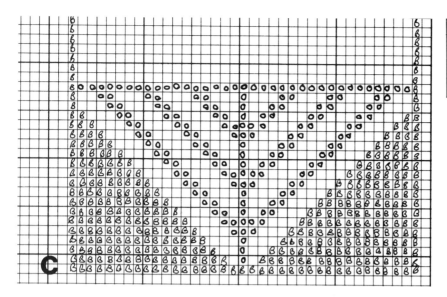

much as the norm. You might be attracted by a design intended for working in tent stitch on canvas; why not work it in cross stitch on linen instead?

The two Chinese motifs shown here are taken from historic canvas-works. They look delightful when stitches in cross stitch on linen.

Another idea is to *graph thematically*. Again and again I am glad that, perhaps many years ago, I took the trouble to graph out a page of, say, 'crowns', which I did not specifically need at the time and for which I could not see any immediate use. However, now I have that page of crowns in my design file and I can constantly refer back to it.

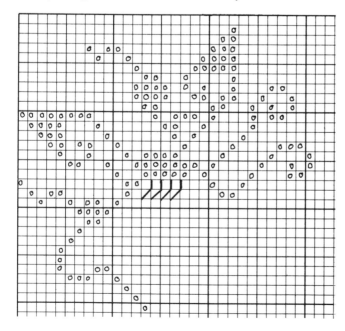

A crab *(left)* and a crane *(opposite)* looking at the sun, symbolising the first official Civil Rank of the Old China paying homage to the emperor.

crab: all indigo
sun: deep yellow
crane:
s   deep yellow
●   dark brown
7   beige

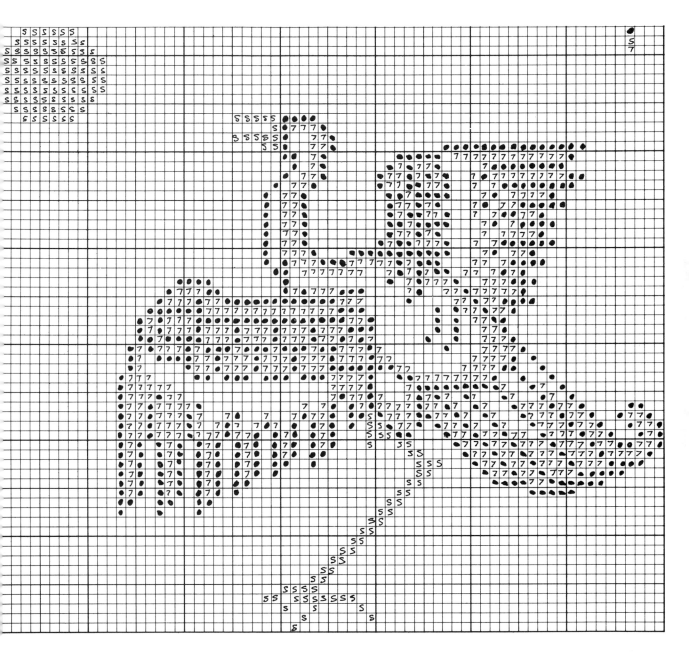

Some of the other ideas you might start thematically collecting in graph form include:

tree shapes

leaf shapes

chair legs

shells

tiles.

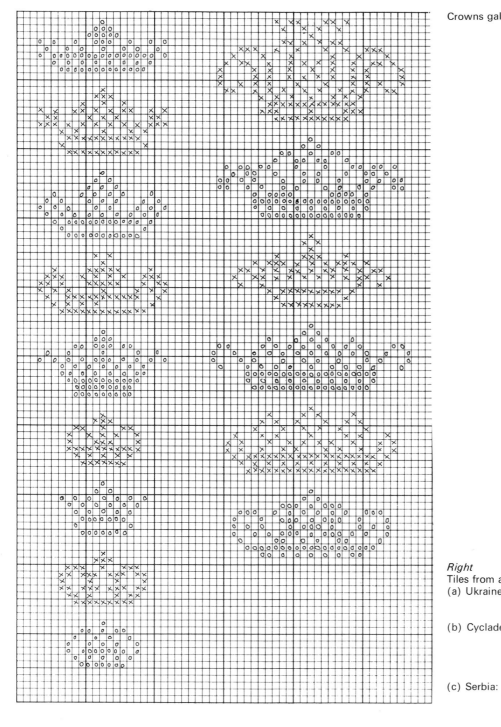

Crowns galore

Right
Tiles from a variety of sources.

(a) Ukraine:	/	red
	○	yellow
	●	blue
(b) Cyclades:	3	blue
	●	black
	○	yellow
	/	red
	≠	green
(c) Serbia:	3	blue
	/	red

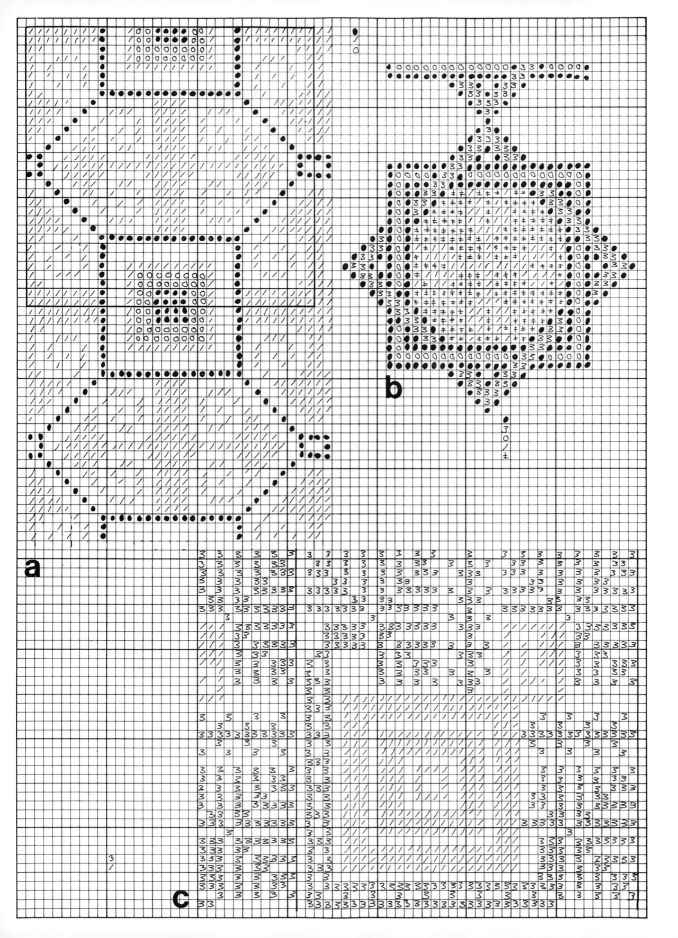

a

b

c

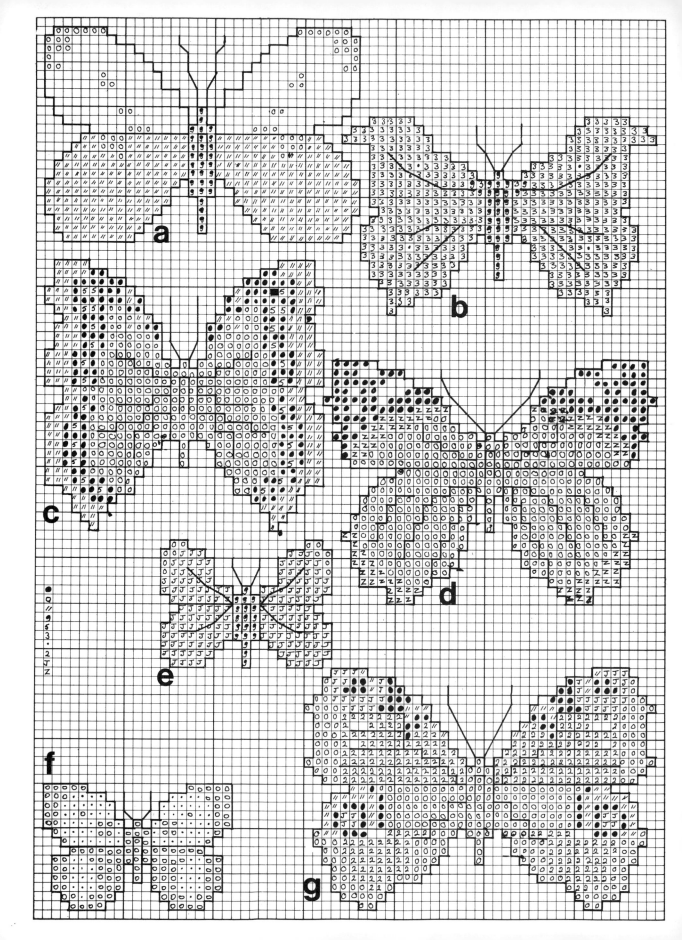

My basic butterflies, used in so many different ways.

. . . and the graphed butterflies can be worked up like this

(a) large white, *Pieris brassicae* (b) brimstone, *Gonepteryx rhamni* (c) mourning cloak (Camberwell beauty) *Nymphalis antiopa* (d) red admiral, *Vanessa atalanta* (e) holly blue, *Celastrina argiolus* (f) gatekeeper, *Pyronia tithonus* and (g) peacock, *Inachis io*.

●	black	2	deep red
○	dark brown	J	pale purple
//	cream	z	bright red
g	grey		(outlined in
5	pale blue		black back
3	yellow		stitch)
·	orange		

I do suggest that you *concentrate on themes that interest you*. I love butterflies. I graphed out seven familiar British garden and hedgerow varieties – and here they are for you to share. (Yes, I keep my page of butterfly shapes in my design file.)

Versatility is important when it comes to doing your own designing. Versatility includes economy. The more you can use a motif the better. I have used my butterflies to the maximum (it took a long time to draw them and I always want to be the most time-effective). Instructions for using the butterfly motifs are on pp. 97–100.

As long as a motif is correctly copied from the original graph it does not matter if its surroundings are changed. I experiment with working motifs

The same butterflies look much better, however, with a leafy background (the circular picture is 17 cm, 6¾ in, in diameter)

either singly, grouped within a circular format or set formally one above
the other. You can see examples of what I mean by looking at the colour
photograph showing my 'butterfly collection'. There is a round picture,
a formal sampler, a long bell pull and a single motif jewellery roll.

I rearranged the butterflies to form my 'butterfly sampler', 25.4 × 14.6 cm (10 × 5¾ in) overall

You will find that you can get an equal number of *different projects from a set of basic motifs*. You can use your 'thematic motifs' for embellishing such items as:

single motifs

coasters

placemats

Handkerchief corners

jewellery rolls

napkins

formal placing of motifs

bell pulls

belt

luggage straps

attractive groupings within circular or similar formats

pictures

photograph albums, scrapbooks or file covers

cushion covers

lingerie sachets.

Surrounds to motifs require a bit of attention. Remember that when you are stitching you must always leave between one motif and another *a number of threads exactly divisible by the size of your stitching.* If you are stitching, say, over 4 threads of fabric you can leave 4, 8 or 12 (and so on) fabric threads between one motif and another. You must not leave 9, 11 or 15. . . .

As well as motifs, I like to 'collect' *background fillers.* You will notice that I have used a small leaf shape for the circular butterfly grouping. First, using a china plate as marker, I tacked the outline of a circle on my linen and stitched butterflies within it. Then, still on the area within that circle, I stitched my favourite leaf shape, shown here, turned variously through 90°, 180° or 270° as I liked. At the circle's circumference the leaves stop. No leaf protrudes on to a butterfly area.

This is the same 'background idea' that I used for the Wesley family tree illustrated on p. 90. You will notice that later leaves and part-leaves join already-worked leaves to form particularly interesting shapes.

So, I have my 'favourite leaf' and I also like the three-grass repeating design I show here. I used this background filler on my butterfly bell pull. Between each butterfly motif I worked a section, picked at random, of the repeating grass pattern. As long as each working adheres to the centre of the whole design, whichever random section you choose will look alright.

You can never, of course, have too many *border patterns.* Wide borders, narrow borders . . . 'collect' as many as possible in your design file. Experiment taking some *through corners.* Look at page 85. I have diagonally divided a simple border pattern in three places, A, B and C. At a corner a design becomes a mirror image of itself; look at the different corner shapes produced, therefore, by turning on a diagonal at A and B and C.

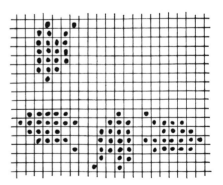

A basic leaf motif can be turned through 90°, 180° or 270° for greatest realism

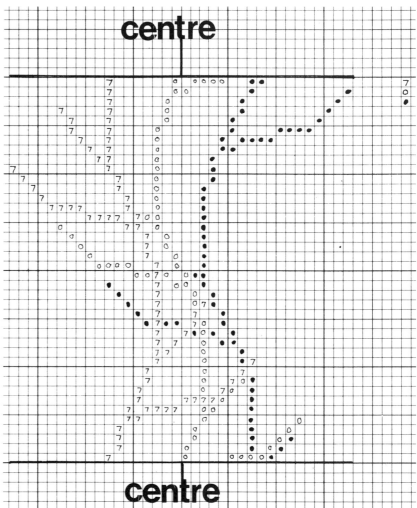

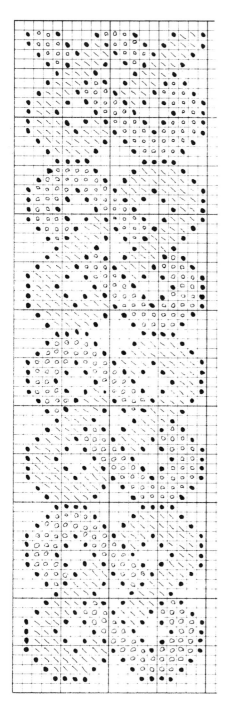

Border design from Stebni Community,
Vyzhnytsya County, Bucovina

I like this background filler (one 'repeat' shown between solid lines). As long as it is correctly centred vertically any part of the design can be employed:

7   lightest green
○   medium green
●   darkest green

Why not graph out a few simple border patterns and mark several diagonals on each one? Form 'corners' at each diagonal. Keep these exercises in your design file as they will remind you how to form corner patterns.

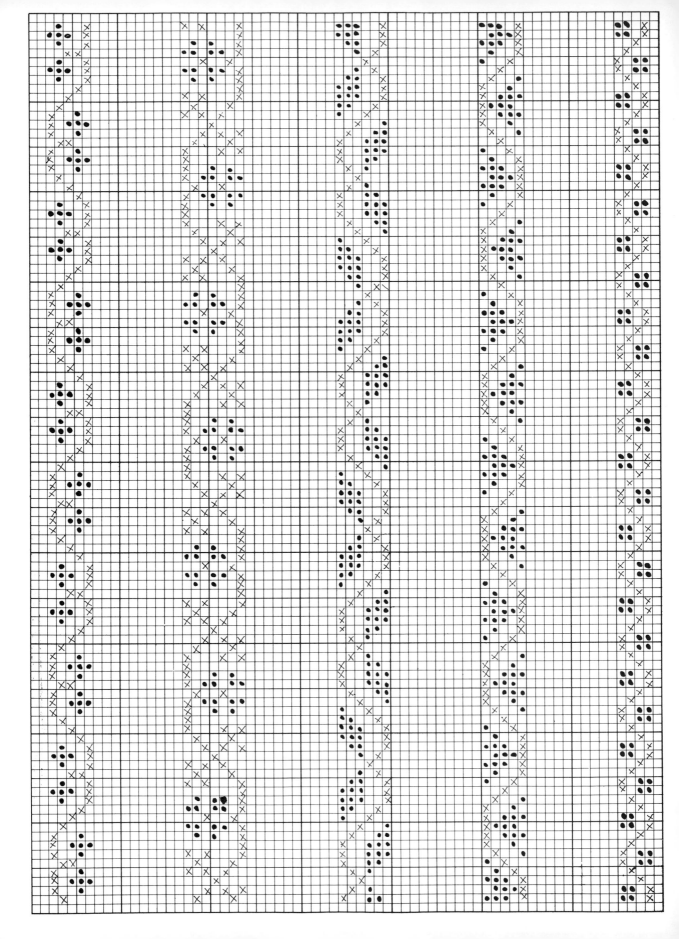

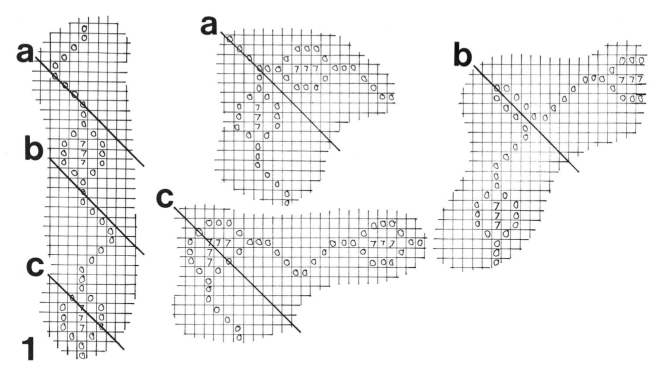

To turn a corner: a simple motif (1) has diagonals drawn at (a), (b) and (c). Different corners are formed from each diagonal

Lettering

Alphabets and numbers occur in so MANY cross stitch designs. Alright, I do admit that gone are the days when we or those we know need to have our underwear and bedlinen cross-stitched with initials and appropriate coronets. And woven and printed nametapes have similarly killed the need for stitched identification. Nonetheless, on samplers and on many other cross stitch pieces you might like to work your own name – or that of the lucky recipient if it is a gift. Here are some alphabet and number styles. *Collect as many alphabets* as you can to provide a special section in your design file.

If you would like books specifically on lettering you might find the following helpful:

Blanche Cirker (ed.), *Needlework Alphabets and Designs*, Dover, 1975, publication of *The Embroiderer's Alphabet, Letters, Figures, Monograms and Ornaments for embroideries on counted thread*, published in France by Editions Th. de Dillmont, n.d.

Rita Weiss (ed.), *Victorian Alphabets, Monograms and Names for Needleworkers*, Dover, 1974, selection of alphabets, names, initials and monograms from *Godey's Lady's Book* and *Peterson's Magazine*, 1852–1880.

Left
Border designs drawn by Professor Julius Lessing during travels in Eastern Europe in 1879

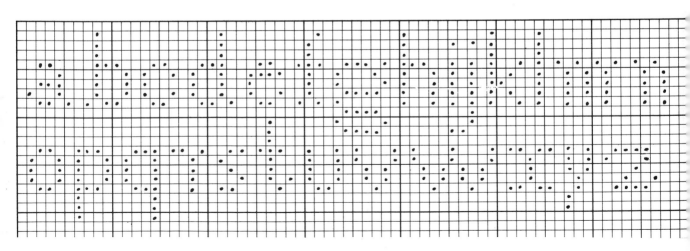

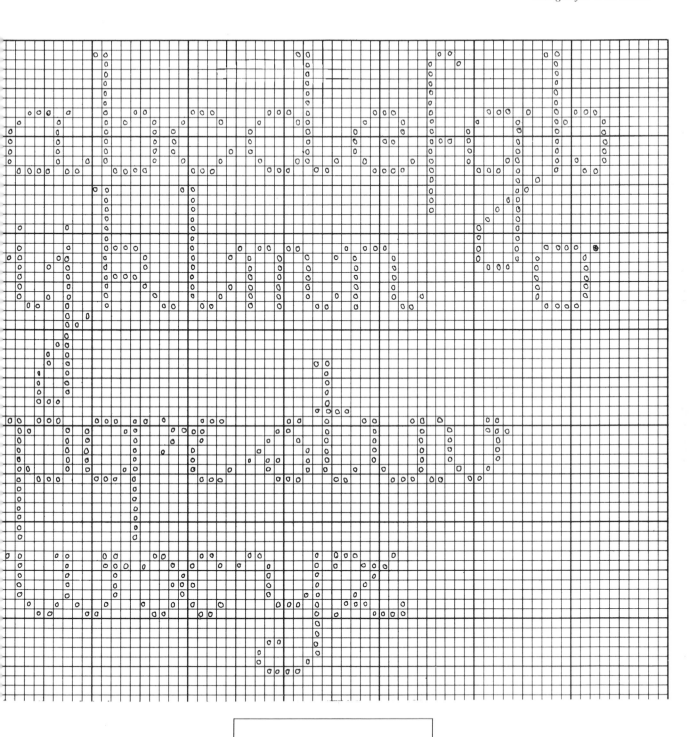

Always leave a needle
threaded. *Then it is easier to
find it when it is lost*

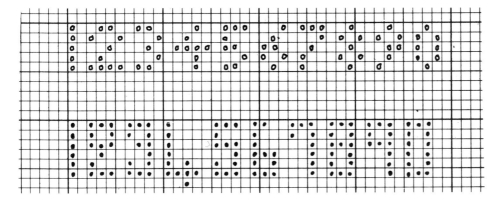

Leisure Arts also publish several leaflets specifically offering charted alphabets and lettering.

You will see that some of the alphabets I give here have *proportional spacing*. Although in the capitalised alphabets all the letters are the same height, 'W' is wider than 'I'. This means that when 'counting to find centre' you must count squares on your graph paper rather than the number of alphabet letters used.

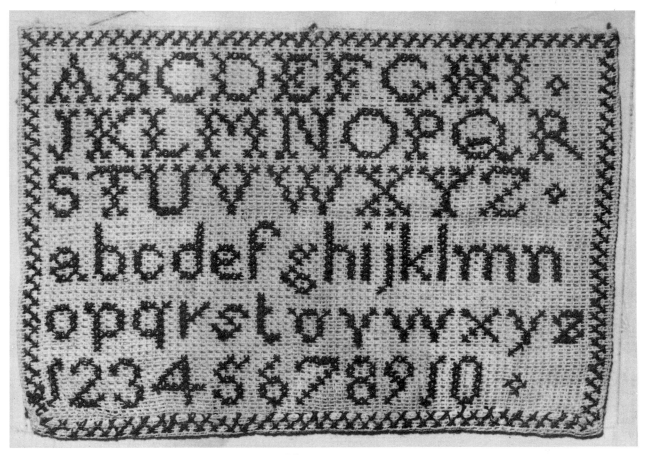

Lettering sampler, 8.5×12.5 cm (3¼×5 in). (*Nancy Hodgkin*)

> *For that really* professional *touch, remember − when making up a cross-stitch piece − carefully to* press *it at each stage of construction*

The Wesley family tree; fruit are formed of velvet stitch. The piece was finished for Carol Wesley's birthday in 1980. Design 21.5 × 15.5 cm (8½ × 6¼ in)

To centre a name or inscription you should first graph out the entire wording. I usually leave three or four squares between words. Including those spaces between words, count how many squares across have been used. If you have used, say, 72 squares across, then the line to the right of the 36th square across marks your vertical central point. You will accordingly subsequently stitch 36 stitches to the left of the centre of your fabric and 36 to the right.

If you have used an *uneven number* of squares, mark the line to the left of the central square. If, say, you have used 71 squares across, mark to the

If you have an uneven vertical square count when centering a name or inscription, mark the vertical centre line to the left of the central square so that you have the extra square (later 'an extra stitch') to the *right* of centre (1). Alternatively you can sometimes add an extra space between words to give an even square count (2)

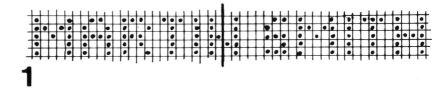

1

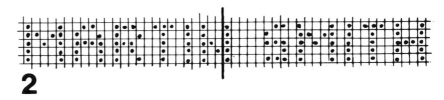

2

line to the left of the 36th square. This will mean that you will stitch 35 stitches to the left of the centre of your fabric and 36 to the right of it.

To put it another way, if you have 'an extra square' or stitch – make sure it ends up to the right of your centre.

If you have used more than one word in your inscription, and if you feel unhappy about having an imbalance, with one extra square-and-stitch to one side of centre, you can, if you have one or three (or five or seven) spaces between words alter the length of those spaces by a count of one. In other words, if you have written 'Ann Jones (i.e. one space, between 'Ann' and 'Jones') you can alter that space by a vertical count of one. If you have left three squares between the words, increase it to four. If you have left four squares between the two words, change it to three or five vertical squares.

This is a form of *compensation* or alteration to achieve overall optical correctness. Another form of lettering compensation is if you have a capital 'R' followed by a capital 'Y'. You might want to move the Y one square closer to the R.

As well as rigid lettering formed of unconnected characters, you might like to try *signature stitching*.

First I signed my name in my normal – usually illegible – handwriting, in pencil on graph paper. Then, using the fluid 'curved line method' (see p. 71) I blocked off relevant squares.

I then stitched from my graph. I surrounded my stitched signature with little flowers worked in colours to complement my summer wardrobe. I wear a lot of lavender so I used an appropriate shade of linen.

Alas, the weft threads of my fabric are much thicker than the warp. This has resulted in a heightening of my design. It would not have mattered in many cases, but since I am stitching my signature it is less realistic than I should have liked.

But I include an illustration so that you can see how a 'stitched signature' looks, and I mention the difficulty as an example not only of the fact that no system is always perfect but to warn *you* to check on warp and weft compatability before you start to 'signature stitch'!

Having difficulty remembering in which direction your 'upper diagonal' should face? Refer constantly to the 'symbolic key' temporarily stitched in an upper corner of your fabric

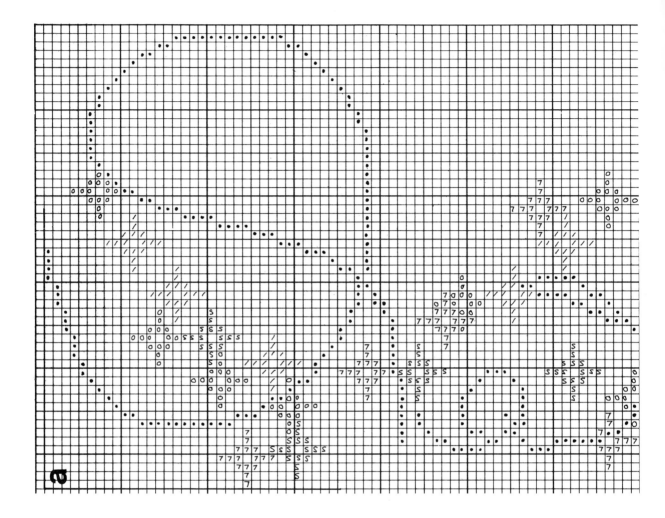

To Make A Signature Pouch You Will Need:

50 cm (19½ in) linen-type fabric (I used a dressmaking fabric with 11 threads per centimetre, 27 threads per inch weft count)

Similar amount of matching lining

48 × 26 cm (19 × 10¼ in) strong stiffener (I used double-mesh, penelope. canvas with 5 holes per cm, 12 per inch)

All-purpose sewing thread, purple

1 strand each DMC 554 (pale mauve), 727 (cream), 444 (yellow), blanc (white), 3371 (black)

Tapestry 22 needle.

First cut a piece of linen 28 cm (11 in) wide. Zigzag all around the edges to prevent fraying.

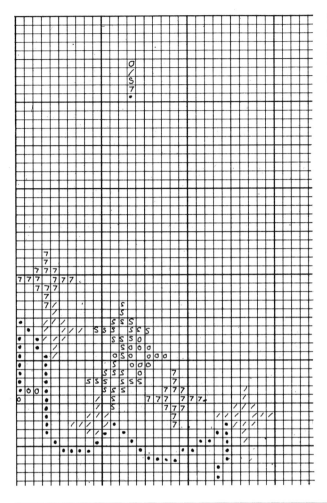

My signature design:

○   white
/   cream
s   yellow
7   pale pink
●   black

Left-handed? Place the book in front of a mirror to be able to follow the diagrams

A personal linen 'clutch', with star-flowers in colours to match your summer outfits
(bag 17×26 cm, 6¾×10¼ in when closed)

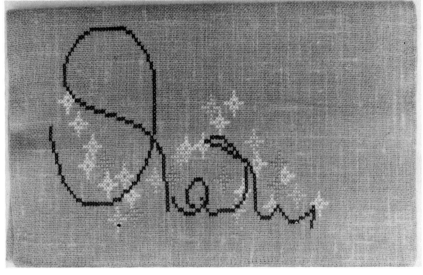

Take a piece of graph paper and lightly pencil your signature – large enough to occupy about 25 cm (10 in) across the paper. Now block in the signature and surround it with little flowers as I have done.

Stitching will be in *2 strands* over *2 linen threads*.

Site your signature so that point A is *3.5 cm* ($1\frac{1}{2}$ in) up from one end of your linen shape and 3.5 cm ($1\frac{1}{2}$ in) in from the left hand edge.

When you have done all the stitching, use my *sandwich make-up method* (opposite), remembering to put in your stiffener before you seal the sandwich.

When you have sealed and stitched the closed 'sandwich', fold up 15 cm (6 in) at the undecorated end of the shape, linings together, and oversew the sides of what will now look like a bag. Fold the stitched end over as flap – and your bag is finished.

Which makes me think it is time for a treasure-store of projects. . . .

Stranded cottons have no nap so you can stitch from either end of your thread

5 Projects and more projects!

You will already have seen some practical ideas placed elsewhere in the book but this chapter is a whole *collection* of projects that can be worn, displayed, given away or kept as heirlooms.

Some are easy, some are more demanding – I just hope that they encourage YOU to 'make' a whole variety of cross stitch treasures.

They are mostly projects that you can easily *finish and make up* yourself. Nothing is more infuriating, I find, than having to spend vast sums of precious money in having a pair of slippers professionally made up, and even if you can find someone to do it for you he will probably take some time over it.

You will see that some of my ideas are made up with what I call my *sandwich method*.

This involves a flat stitched area with same-sized lining; it is simple to do and when you have mastered the knack of making a presentable sandwich you will find it is a very versatile making up technique.

To Execute a Sandwich Makeup You Will Need:

An area of fabric already cross-stitched (make sure that all your tackings are removed)

A similar area of lining

Gütermann thread to match

Place the fabric and lining shapes right sides together, making sure that warp and weft threads are in alignment. Machine or hand stitch 1 cm ($\frac{1}{2}$ in) around all edges, leaving 8 cm (3 in) on a small item, to 12 cm ($4\frac{1}{2}$ in) on a larger item, unstitched, somewhere in the middle of one edge or end.

Snip the surplus at the corners almost – but not quite – to the stitching.

Turn the fabric right sides out. Push the corners as close to 90° as possible. Tack around all round edges and machine or hand saddle-stitch 3 mm ($\frac{1}{8}$ in) around the whole shape. This will 'hold' the turned in fabric at the opening, although if you feel happier you can oversew this opening.

When you have mastered the plain sandwich you might like to try some *sandwich varieties*:

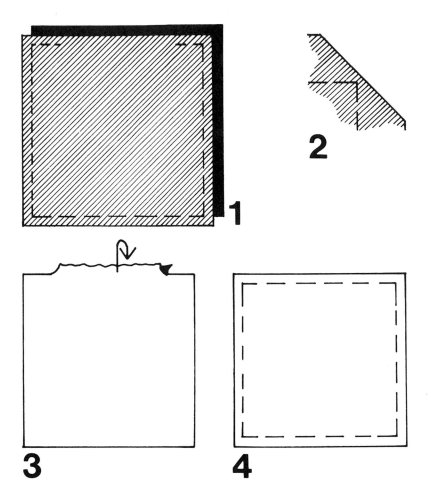

Basic sandwich method (wrong side of fabric shaded): fabric and (black) backing are stitched together, with a gap left (1). Surplus is removed almost to the corners (2). The shape is turned right side out and the surplus turned in (3) and saddle-stitching keeps the sandwich shape flat and secures the opening (4)

1 *Padded or stiffened sandwich.* Some items (such as my 'signature bag') need stiffening. In addition to the fabric and lining you will need an area stiffening 2 cm ($\frac{7}{8}$ in) shorter and narrower than the main fabric and lining. I often use strong canvas as stiffener. It holds its shape well and it is not difficult subsequently to machine stitch through the canvas when the finished sandwich is saddle-stitched.

When you stitch fabric and lining together, leave nearly all of one of the shortest sides unstitched. Turn the two fabrics right sides out and push the corners to their 90°. Then, before folding in the opening surpluses, insert the stiffener – and proceed as before.

2 *Circular sandwich.* This is made in the same manner as a square or rectangular sandwich except that you have to make small V-shaped cuts in the surplus before you turn the fabrics right sides out. These V-shaped cuts, almost but not quite to the stitching, accommodate excess surplus.

3 *Irregularly-shaped sandwich.* As with a round or oval sandwich, make V-cuts in the surplus around a convex part of the stitching but also make

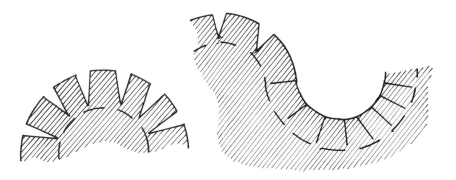

Before turning a round or oval sandwich right sides out, make V-slits in the surplus. With an irregularly-shaped sandwich make 'V' or straight slits depending on the curve

simple cuts around concave parts of the shape. These cuts will ease all surpluses when the sandwich is turned right side out.

☆☆☆☆☆☆☆☆☆

You can try the sandwich method when making a drinks coaster or a bell-pull.

My bell-pull is decorated with butterflies from my design file (see p. 78). You can also see it in colour.

To Make My Butterfly Bell-Pull You Will Need:

Area evenweave 92 × 12 cm (36 × 4¾ in)

92 × 12 cm (36 × 4¾ in) lining. (I used lightweight calico)

Two wooden dowels with end knobs, 10 cm (4 in) minimum width between dowel knobs

All-purpose sewing thread, cream

1 skein each DMC 961 (dark rose), 211 (lavender), 986 (dark green), 704 (pale green), 906 (bright green), 799 (pale blue), 606 (scarlet), 970 (orange), 444 (yellow), 3371 (black), 3031 (brown), 822 (beige), 452 (grey).

Tapestry 24 needle.

First tack a central line from top to bottom of the linen. Then stitch whichever butterfly (look at p. 78) you like. I personally chose to site one butterfly immediately beneath another, both centred on my tacked line, and another butterfly centred below that, and so on. My top butterfly is *7.5 cm (3 in)* from the top of the fabric. Stitching is with *2 strands over 2 fabric* threads.

I first of all stitched a *gatekeeper*, the top of its head 8 cm (3⅛ in) – measuring down the tacking – from the top of my linen. I then counted down *threads* from the bottom of that butterfly, and *20 clear threads down* I stitched a *holly blue*. I then left another 20 threads clear and worked a *mourning cloak*, another 20 threads and a *large white*, another 20 clear threads and a *brimstone*, another 20 down to the *peacock*, 20 clear threads down to the *red admiral*. Another 20 threads down and I was ready for my second *gatekeeper*, and so on. I stitched each butterfly twice.

You can see the colours I used by checking with the graph's caption. I tried to get each butterfly as nearly realistic as I could.

When you have worked all the butterflies, stitch any sections you like of my repeating 'background filler' on p. 83. You have three different greens. There are three colours indicated on the repeating background filler graph. It does not matter which shade of green you use for which symbol on the graph. It does not matter WHERE on the repeating graph design you start stitching as long as:

1 Each section worked is appropriately 'centred' to your tacking, and
2 Your vertical colour alignment never alters from one space between butterflies to another. I had my palest green to the left throughout, my bright green in the middle and my darkest green on the right.

Remove the tacking, and attach the fabric to the lining by the sandwich method I have just described. Turn the top 3 cm ($1\frac{1}{4}$ in) of the linen shape over to the lining side and hem to the lining, leaving the sides unattached as illustrated. Similarly turn and attach the lower 3 cm ($1\frac{1}{4}$ in) of your shape. Press.

You can now put the dowel hangers through these two retainers formed by the turned-back ends.

✭✭✭✭✭✭✭✭✭

Rather than use the sandwich method I preferred a *drawn thread* construction when designing my butterfly jewellery roll.

I chose a *red admiral* from the graph on p. 78 but you could stitch another butterfly if you prefer.

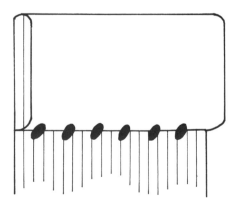

When you have made the bell-pull into a long sandwich turn the top 3 cm ($1\frac{1}{4}$ in) over and hem it to the lining (here striped)

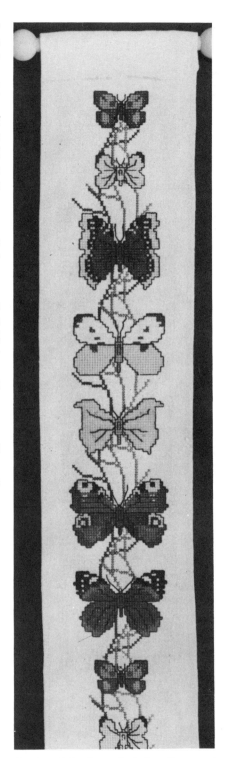

Section of the 'butterfly bell-pull', 10.5 cm ($4\frac{1}{4}$ in) across

Butterfly jewellery roll, 23.7 cm (9¼ in) wide

To Make a Butterfly Jewellery Roll You Will Need:

Area evenweave 27×35.5 cm ($10\frac{1}{4} \times 14$ in)

Two pieces of white satin, one 33×24 cm ($13 \times 9\frac{1}{2}$ in), one 8×24 cm ($3\frac{1}{4} \times 9\frac{1}{2}$ in)

8 cm (3 in) narrow white satin ribbon (you may prefer to make this from another scrap of white satin)

50 cm ($19\frac{1}{2}$ in) each narrow satin ribbon, black and scarlet

1 silver popper fastener

All-purpose sewing thread (white and cream)

1 skein each DMC 606 (scarlet), 3371 (black), 3031 (brown) – if you would rather stitch another butterfly, choose appropriate colours.

Tapestry 24 needle.

First I prepared a linen 'mat'. 2 cm ($\frac{3}{4}$ in) in from each of the four edges of my linen I withdrew 4 warp or weft threads. I mitred the corners, the tip

99

of the corner being 8-threads-diagonal count from the junction of the withdrawals. I turned the edges' surplus under and hemmed. On the inner side of the withdrawals I worked drawn-thread hemming.

I now had an edged 'mat' on which to cross stitch, on the *right* side of the mat. I stitched with *2 strands* over *2 fabric threads*.

The butterfly is worked, antennae at the top, in the bottom left-hand corner of the 'mat' if you hold it 'landscape style', that is shortways up. The bottom of the butterfly's body is 3.8 cm (1½ in) up from the bottom withdrawal and the same distance in from the left-hand vertical withdrawal.

After you have worked all the cross stitching, execute small running stitches with 1 strand of black to attach the ribbons, black on top of red, at the horizontal centre of the mat, 5 cm (2 in) in from the left vertical withdrawal, roughly above the butterfly.

Don't forget to strip *(the thread, that is). Pull out one strand and then another and lay as many strands together to achieve smoother, untwisted stitching*

The outside of the jewellery roll is prepared as a linen mat. The butterfly is sited so that it rests 3.8 cm (1½ in) up and in from withdrawals (black lines). Ribbons are attached with a single vertical line of tiny running stitches (arrowed)

Now you can prepare the satin lining. First take the smaller area of satin and work narrow hems around all four edges. Hem one long and the two short sides to the large satin and form 'compartments' with little running stitches. Sew one end of the ribbon to the satin, one half of the

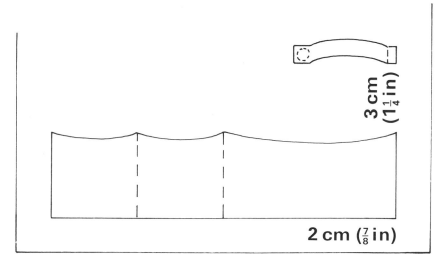

3 cm (1¼ in)

2 cm (⅞ in)

After all four edges of the smaller satin shape are turned under and hemmed, it is placed on the large satin and hemmed along one long and both shorter sides. Compartments are formed by running stitches. A length of satin ribbon is sewn and attached by a popper to hold necklaces

popper to the unattached end of the ribbon and the other half of the popper to the satin.

Place the satin lining on the wrong side of the linen mat. Turn under the edges of the satin so that they just extend to the inside of the linen withdrawals and neatly hem around all four edges.

Perfect for the *déjeuner à deux* . . . placemats with modern art cross stitching. (*The china is Exeter by Jonelle*)

Modern Art Placemats

You could use the same mat construction for *modern art placemats*. I designed a pair of such mats: You can also see them photographed in

colour. Each mat has a copy of a geometric artwork in the left-hand upper corner.

What a lovely 'wedding present' idea . . . copy two art works that you know mean something to the recipients.

Similarly, you could work two mats with designs *all in dark red* for a ruby wedding present. You could work appropriately-coloured mats for other anniversaries. And if you like the idea of 'modern art stitching' you could work more than a mere pair . . . a dozen placemats to provide conversational starters at your dinner party.

There are no strict instructions here. I suggest you go to your local museum or gallery and buy postcards that inspire you.

As well as appropriate colours of stranded cotton *for each pair of mats you will need*:

30 cm (11 in) evenweave linen

Graph paper and coloured pens or pencils

All-purpose sewing thread (cream)

Tapestry 24 needle.

Prepare each mat from a linen shape 30 × 38 cm (11 × 15 in) with 3 withdrawn threads 2.5 cm (1 in) in from each edge, corners then mitred and surplus folded under and hemmed.

When you have prepared the mats, you can *graph out* your chosen design, and transpose it in cross stitches to the linen mats. I stitched each motif, upper left-hand corner 1 cm (just under ½ in) down and in from withdrawals, upper left-hand corner of the mat.

> *Always leave a needle* threaded. *Then it is easier to find it when it is lost*

And now, time for a bit of Christmas table festivity. . . .

Scandinavians, in particular, have such lovely 'special Christmas' decorations. We had some friends coming in for a Boxing Day buffet, and I wanted to make my smoked glass oval dining table (from Italy, via John Lewis) look specially festive, so I designed a bright red table runner and matching cocktail or buffet napkins.

To Make the Runner and Ten Napkins You Will Need:

38 cm (15 in) red Aida, 150 cm (60 in) wide, 6 blocks per centimetre (15 per inch)

All-purpose sewing thread (red)

3 skeins DMC blanc (white)

Tapestry 22 needle.

First cut an entire width of fabric 20 cm (8 in) high. From this area cut off a 105 cm (41 in) width to give you the main runner. From the remainder

For Christmas, a set of festive table runner and mats. (*Wooden pieces from Hawaii*)

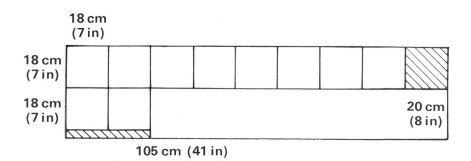

Cutting diagram for Christmas table runner and napkins (surplus shaded)

of this width cut two 18 × 18 cm (7 × 7 in) squares for two of the napkins. From the other width, 18 cm (7 in) high, cut eight more squares.

Fray (unravel) 2 blocks deep around all edges of all shapes. Machine zigzag, with the red thread, just inside all the fringing around all edges (I found my Frister + Rossmann stitched best with stitch length 1 and stitch width 2). Tack a central line from one end to the other of the runner.

Now prepare to cross stitch – *2 strands* over *1 fabric block*. At either end of the runner work two angels so that stitch A is *12 blocks up* from the end of the runner and *6 blocks over* from the central line. The angels should face the centre.

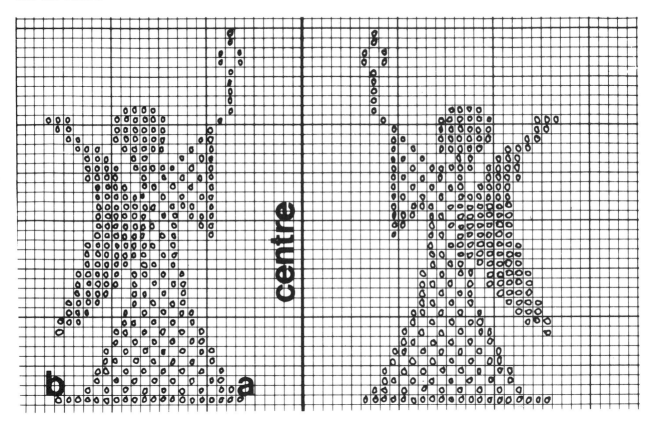

When you have worked four angels on the runner, remove the tacking.

Stitch an angel in one corner of each of your napkins. Here, stitch so that B is *12 blocks up* and *12 blocks over* from the corner. Make sure all the napkin angels are facing in the same direction.

✰✰✰✰✰✰✰✰✰✰

Other ideas spring to mind as a result of this project:

1 You could make a *butterfly cocktail/buffet set* using a pale blue Aida and some of the butterfly motifs shown on p. 78.

2 The little angel shape shown above could be worked on red Aida to produce Christmas tablemats – see p. 101.

And at your Christmas party you might even want to wear your hostess apron with the cross-stitched rose design (see p. 131).

Perhaps a young man of distinction might appreciate a *Humpty Dumpty sweater* as a Christmas (or general) present?

I don't know about you, but I find it jolly difficult to think of something exciting, worthwhile and masculine to embroider for a growing young man!

This Humpty Dumpty has a cross stitch body and long knitted legs. Sensibly, he is attached by touch-and-close fastening so that he can be removed when the sweater is washed.

For that really professional *touch, remember – when making up a cross-stitch piece – carefully to* press *it at each stage of construction*

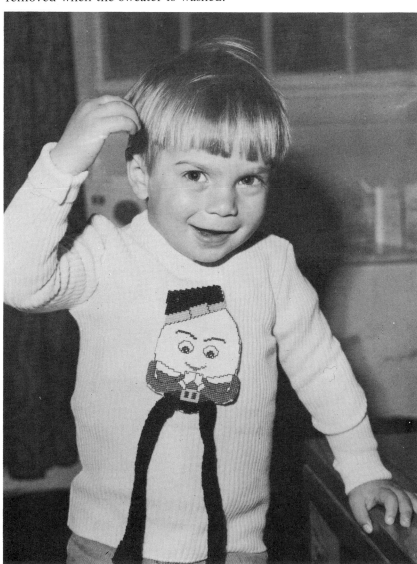

Julian Wharton holds his head up! His sweater has a cross-stitched Humpty Dumpty with knitted legs. Humpty, who can easily be removed for washing, is 12 cm (4¾ in) tall. (*Sweater from Marks & Spencer*)

To Make Humpty You Will Need:

Area evenweave linen 20 × 15 cm (8 × 6 in)

1 skein each DMC 666 (red), 796 (blue), 444 (yellow), 3371 (black), 435 (brown)

Tapestry 22 needle
and, to complete him . . .

Off-white sweater to fit the Young Man

Area white felt 13 × 9 cm (5 × 3½ in)

Area firm iron-on interfacing 13 × 9 cm (5 × 3½ in)

Strip white touch-and-close fastening 1 cm (⅜ in) wide, 7 cm (2¾ in) long

Small amount of 4-ply black knitting wool

Small amount of cotton wool or other padding

Pair size 9 knitting needles

All-purpose sewing thread (white)

Sharply-pointed sewing needle

Humpty Dumpty's face and body:
7   black
○   yellow
●   brown
/   blue
s   red
    outlined in
    dark blue
    back stitch

First prepare the body, cross and back stitched on linen according to the graph – *2 strands* over *2 linen threads*.

Knit two legs, both the same:

1st row: cast on 12 stitches and knit ten rows stocking stitch

11th row: Knit to last 2 stitches, knit 2 together

12th row: Purl to last 2 stitches, purl 2 together

Now continue, on 10 stitches, until entire leg measures 18 cm (7 in). Cast off.

Stitch up both legs by joining the long back seam and bottom of the foot to form a long floppy 'sack'.

Press the iron-on interfacing to the reverse of the decorated area of linen. This will prevent cut threads fraying.

Cut to just under 1 cm (⅓ in) of surplus all round the edge of the body shape. Make little 'V's to accommodate curves (the 'V's almost but not quite to the edge of the stitched area). Turn the surplus under and hold in place with tackings.

Cut an area of felt to match that of Humpty's body. Stitch one of the two halves of the touch-and-close fastening to the white felt. Pin the knitted legs in place on the reverse of the main body shape (1.25 cm, ½ in, in to the body shape). Overstitch all around the edges of the body-and-felt shapes with a double thickness of white thread; when you get to the legs, work small back stitches through body shape, legs and felt. (You can later disguise this stitching with a few cover-up herringbone stitches.)

Stitch the other half of the touch-and-close to the sweater. Remove any tackings – and Humpty is all ready to sit on his sweater!

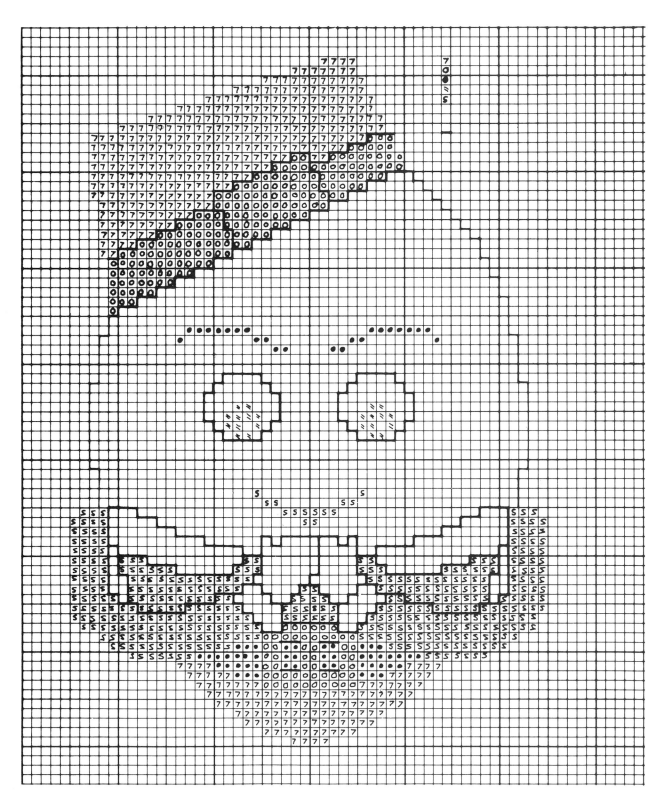

You have already read about the charming *bag-belt* that I saw in Mexico recently (see p. 54). As soon as I got back from Mexico City I designed and made my own.

The belt consists of nine attached pockets, open at the tops. Each bag is 7.5 cm (3 in) wide; if you are narrow waisted you could make eight rather than nine pockets. The same cross stitch pattern is worked on the front and back of each pocket.

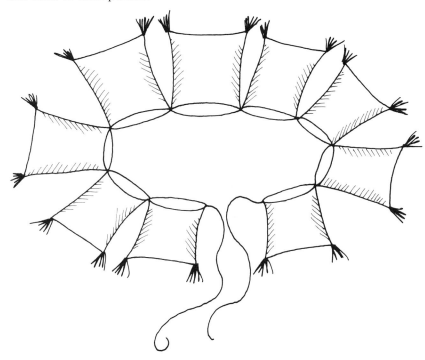

Mexican bag-belt. Each open-topped bag measures 10 × 7.6 cm (4 × 3 in)

Traditionally the Mexican bag-belt should be worked in scarlet on white or natural linen. As such, I find it makes a really useful art accessory, as I can store brushes and pencils in the pockets. And as it is so bright and colourful I can wear it over black silk trousers and matching camisole as a 'hostess apron', useful for holding my handkerchief and other small items during evening entertaining.

This is a versatile project. Make it up in hessian as a gardening apron . . . make the pockets in different-coloured cloth as a harlequin apron for a child. And what a lovely present it would make.

To Make the Mexican Bag-Belt You Will Need:

30 cm (11¾ in) evenweave linen

The same area of lining (I used cotton lawn)

All-purpose sewing thread (white)

9 skeins DMC 666 (red)

Sharp pointed sewing needle

Tapestry 22 needle.

First form nine pockets. Each pocket is formed by stitching AB and BA joined – *2 strands* over *3 fabric threads*.

Each pocket is formed of **ab** repeated as **ba**. When finished, the pocket is folded at **b** so that decoration is on the front and back of the piece

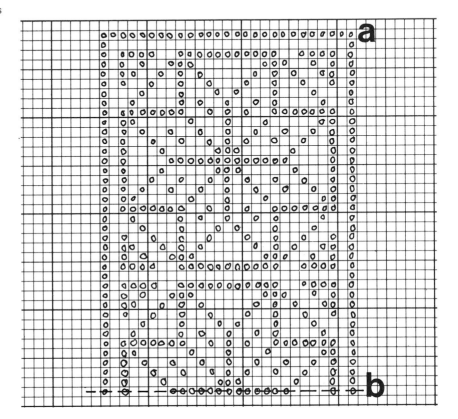

When you have finished all nine pockets' cross stitching, use the simple sandwich method (p. 95) to form nine sandwiches. Work long-legged cross stitch edge binding (2 strands) along both shorter ends of each shape. Fold the shapes in half and oversew (white thread) each side of the resulting 'pockets'. Work long-legged cross stitch edge binding along these sides.

I used my American Express card to form 18 tassels: I wrapped all six strands of the Lystra ten times round the card, short rather than long measurement, and bound the tassel, before cutting it, in the usual way (p. 110.)

Attach one tassel to each lower corner of the pockets. Attach the pockets one to another with small oversewing at the top of each shape. Make two twisted cords 50 cm (just over 19 in) long. Attach one end to each 'end' of the joined pocket shapes to form waist ties.

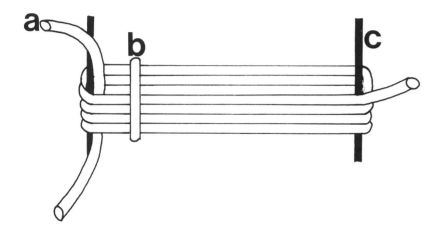

Each pocket has two attached tassels. You can form them around a credit card or around two pencils (here black). Another thread (A) is put through the loops, which are then tightly bound (B). Cut the loops at C to produce an open-ended tassel, which can be attached with thread A

How about a *personalised tie* for the man of the house?

Making ties can be an expensive business as they have to be cut on the cross of the fabric. I have worked out a method of making a tie that requires *only 40 cm (16 in) of fabric!*

I made my husband's tie in russet linen with attractive embroidered stripes formed of his initials, 'MFG', in dark blue, with mustard bands either side.

To Make the Tie You Will Need:

40 cm (16 in) linen (I used a dressmaking linen 140 cm, 55 in, wide)

About 25 cm (10 in) square of appropriate lining fabric

Graph paper

All-purpose sewing thread (russet)

1 skein each DMC 791 (dark blue) and 422 (mustard)
Tapestry 24 needle.

First take a large sheet of newspaper or plain paper and, following the diagram given here, prepare a full-sized paper pattern.

Now stitch your width of fabric, wefts together, to form a long tube, the selvedges at the open ends. Press the seam open. Wrap the paper pattern around it and cut out a tie shape. Zigzag around all the edges to prevent them fraying and tack centrally from one end of the tie shape to the other.

Take your graph paper and sketch out a suitable monogram. You will see that I have graphed my 'MFG' occupying a total of 13 squares up by 15 squares across. Block in a band above and beneath your initials as I have done.

Find the vertical centre of your monogram; if you have forgotten how to do this you will find instructions on p. 91. You should also find the horizontal centre by the same method.

> *Having difficulty remembering in which direction your 'upper diagonal' should face? Refer constantly to the 'symbolic key' temporarily stitched in an upper corner of your fabric*

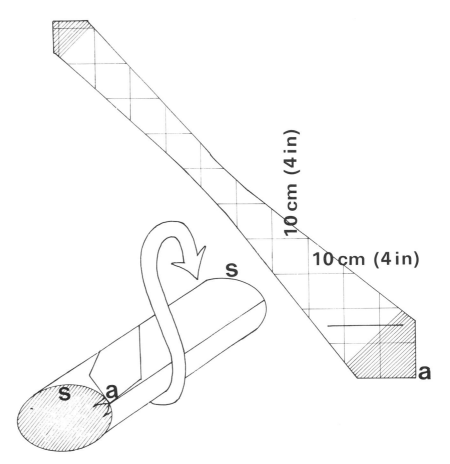

10 cm (4 in)

10 cm (4 in)

Martin Gostelow's personalised tie

Cutting diagram for the tie (lining area shaded). After the fabric has been sewn as a tube (S=selvedge), the tie's paper pattern is wrapped diagonally around it and a fabric shape cut

The monogram for my husband's tie. Lines mark the vertical and horizontal centres of one monogram to show the 'hub':

●   dark blue
7   mustard

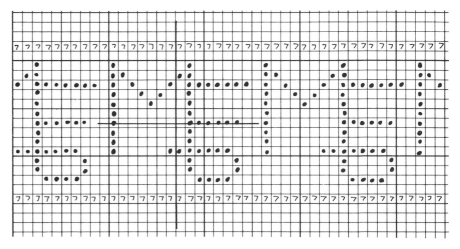

Now you are ready to stitch. All cross stitches will be worked in *2 strands* over *4 linen threads.*

You will find that you have a constructional seam somewhere around the middle of the wider, front, end of your tie shape. Start by stitching a mustard band that *covers this seam,* the hub of your monogram, on the tacking. Stitch a complete monogram and continue stitching monograms either side to about *the outer 2 cm (nearly 1 in) of the tie shape.* Leave these edge areas unstitched.

I worked two complete stripes, with 5 cm (2 in) between stripes. Then I removed my tacking.

I suggest you then cut lining shapes for the ends of the tie as indicated by the shaded area of the illustration. Stitch the sides and ends of the tie and lining shapes, right sides together, and turn them right side out. Press. Fold the tie right sides together and machine stitch from one lined area to the other.

Use a long tube-turner to turn the tie right side out. Hand stitch the final seam joins. Press carefully – and your personalised tie is ready.

✩✩✩✩✩✩✩✩✩✩

How about the *kaftan of a lifetime*?

As you can see from the illustration opposite, I made my kaftan in a deep purple cotton poplin, polyester and cotton mixture, with applied pink linen-mixture yoke panel embellished with typical Middle Eastern motifs in deep purple and cream with gold thread cross stitches.

To Make the Kaftan You Will Need:

A simple kaftan pattern to fit. Make sure it is a pattern with a simple rounded neckline, vertical front neck opening about 22 cm, 9 in, deep (I used Butterick 3384, size 8)

Deep purple poplin as specified on the pattern (I used a polyester and cotton mixture 115 cm, 45 in, wide)

Area of pink linen mixture 45 × 40 cm (18 × 16 in). I used dressmaking fabric, 15 threads per centimetre (40 per inch)

All-purpose sewing thread (pink and purple)

3 skeins each DMC 550 (purple) and 727 (cream)

1 reel Gütermann Metallic Effect Thread (W391): in the US ask for Japanese Metallic yarn (gold)

Tapestry 22 needle.

Cut out front and back dress shapes and front and back neck facing shapes but *do not cut vertical neck openings.* Place these shapes to one side while you embroider.

Following the chart, work the cross stitch decoration on the pink fabric – either *2 strands of purple* or *2 strands of cream threaded with one thickness of gold* – all over *4 fabric threads.*

Left-handed? Place the book in front of a mirror to be able to follow the diagrams

Mary Gostelow's kaftan

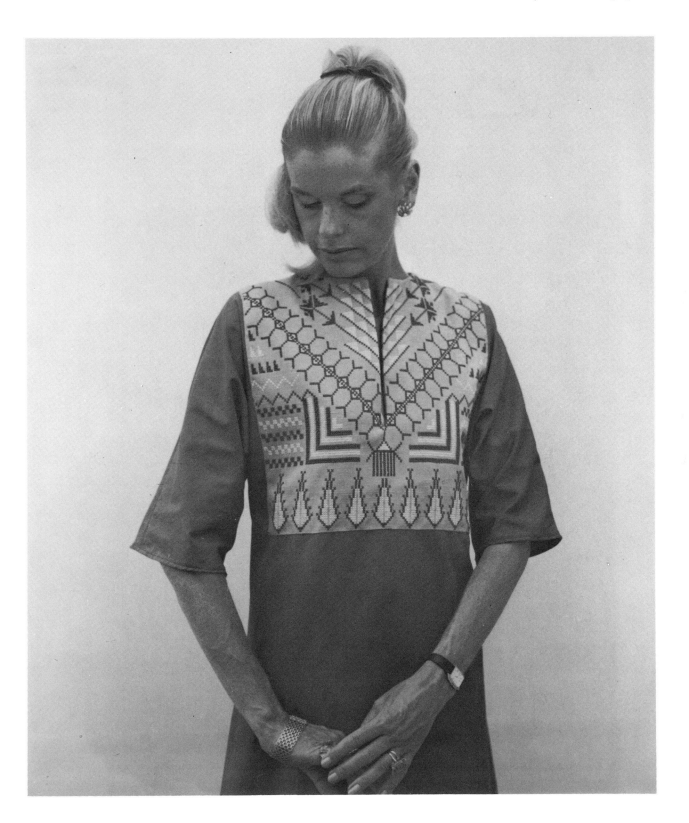

centre

Stitching diagram for my kaftan's applied yoke panel.
○ dark purple
⌐ cream and gold

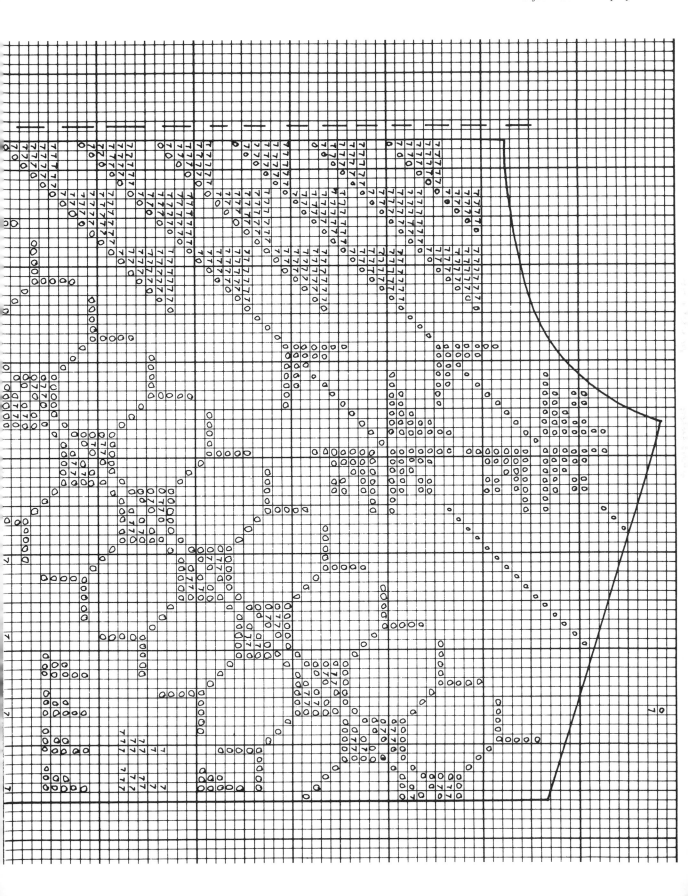

When you have finished embroidering, cut to 2 cm ($\frac{3}{4}$ in) of all outer edges of embroidery. Turn back the surplus at the base and sides of the panel. Tack. Lay the panel on the upper yoke of the right side of the front dress shape, and machine stitch the base and sides of the panel (pink thread).

Work tackings exactly following both sides and base of the neck slit. These will be 'indicators' when you come to attach the facings.

Stitch the shoulder seams of the front and back shapes of the dress and yoke panel, right sides together. Press. Turn the garment right side out.

Attach front and back neck facings. Lay the facings on the main garment, right sides together. Sew around neck and down both sides and across base of vertical neck opening. (Work from the wrong side of the main garment and you can carefully follow your 'indicator' tackings.)

Cut the neck slit, with diagonal corner slits. Cut off surplus fabric at corners at top of the neck slit. Make V slits in the surplus around the neck. Turn the garment right sides out. Tack around the neck and opening, and press.

Now continue making up your garment in your usual dressmaking manner. Stitch underarm and side seams, strengthening the underarm areas with lengths of tape or ribbon.

✬✬✬✬✬✬✬✬✬✬

I hope you enjoy wearing your kaftan as much as I do mine!

There are many variations on this particular theme:

1 How about working a white kaftan, with white linen applied panel and white and silver and/or gold embroidery? What a wedding dress that would be!

2 I should like to see it worked in striking black-and-white . . .

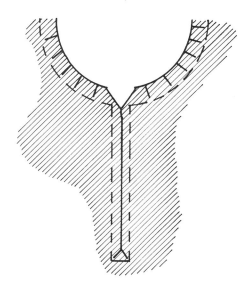

Stitch the neck facings to the main garment, right sides together. (Wrong side shown here, shaded.) Cut off corners' surplus and make surplus neck slits almost to the stitching. Make diagonal slits at the base of the neck to facilitate turning the right side out

Right
Angular geometrics from (a) Lithuania (b) Corfu (c) Azerbaijan and (d) the Yao.
Lithuania: all red
Corfu: /   red
                ●   black
Azerbaijan: ●   black
                7   purple
Yao: all yellow

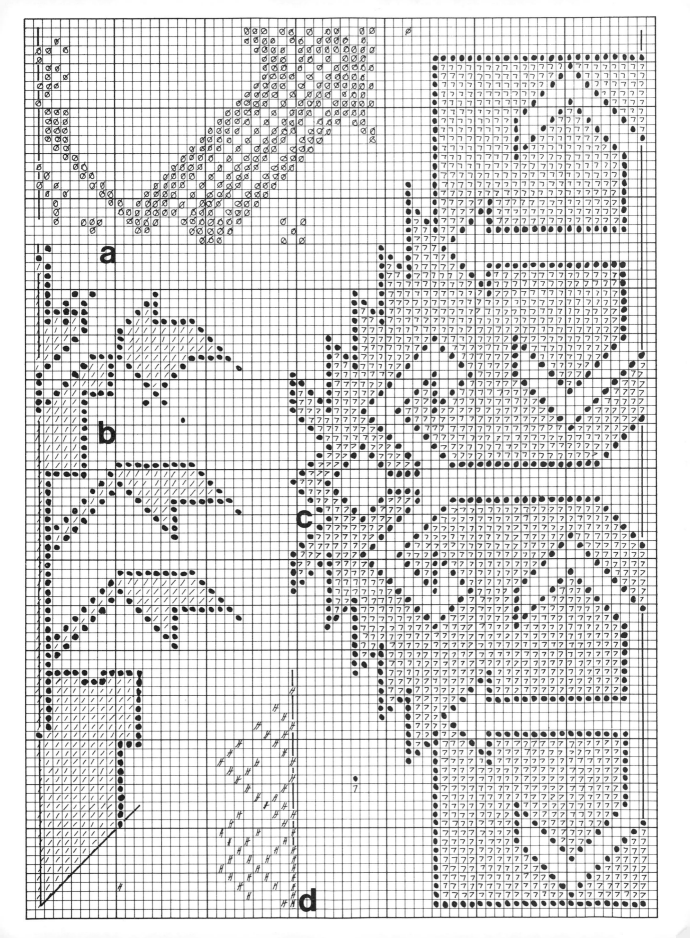

6 How to look after cross stitch

As a needlework designer and teacher I find I get more direct questions about cleaning, blocking, mounting and display than about any other aspects of cross stitch.

I shall therefore turn this chapter into a symposium – and I hope that I have answered all *your* questions too.

Q: I have finished my cross stitch piece. It is filthy. Can I wash it?
A: That depends on what fabric you have used. I wash my all-linen samplers. If you have been working either on a lush material and/or with metallic thread content I would avoid washing.

Before you immerse your piece in water I do suggest that you do a 'spot test' on the reverse to check for colour-running (bleeding). Take a moistened Q-tip or cotton wool ball and carefully press it to an area of each different colour thread used. Has any colouring come off on the cotton wool? If so, you must NOT wash the piece.

I recommend a cold water wash. Particularly in Britain we are sometimes horrified by the idea of washing in *cold water*. How can cold water get things clean?

Well, a short time ago I started doing even my machine laundry in a cold water wash. I now save on energy costs and my laundry takes half the time it used to. And, what is MOST important, my 'whites' are as pristine as ever.

After taking the precautions outlined above, you can certainly feel confident about washing your treasured sampler in a cold water wash. You will find that there are no problems with shrinking or matting, and many washing agents contain a softening ingredient to retain the 'feel' of the fabric you are washing.

(In America some people now prefer Orvus washing paste as its chemical makeup is said to be least harmful to fabrics and threads in the long run. Orvus is available mostly from tack shops and saddlers.)

If you are using a commercial cold water wash you should follow the instructions on the packet carefully. If you prefer NOT to wash in cold water you can use lukewarm water into which you have squeezed a few drops of washing-up liquid.

Carefully immerse the piece and hand-ladle water over it as if you were

Stranded cottons have no nap so you can stitch from either end of your thread

bathing a baby. Do not rub and do not squeeze. Use lots of rinses until the water is absolutely clear.

If your piece is of manageable size you can lay it on a clean bath towel and carefully roll the towel into a sausage shape. Leave it rolled for half an hour to get rid of excess water. Then lay the piece face up, flat, on another clean towel or on an area of blotting paper until it is completely dry; avoid excess heat or light while it is drying.

If, however, you are dealing with a large table cloth, and there is no room to dry it flat, I suggest you cover a length of your washing line with a clean towel. Over this hang the item to be dried. Move it at regular intervals (say every half hour), changing the 'crease line' to avoid permanent creasing when the cloth is eventually dry.

If you are dealing with clothing, I suggest that where possible you dry items spread out flat on a towel.

Q: Overall my work is clean but I have one grease spot on it. What can I do about this?
A: I swear by Goddard's 'Dry Clean', a spot-lifter that I never travel without. I have used it successfully on many of my cross-stitched pieces. I should stress, however, that I have not been stitching for centuries and centuries, so the long term effects of the chemical application contained in such a spot-lifter have not been practically tested.

Q: Why don't you recommend simply taking the dirty piece of work to the dry cleaners?
A: Lucky you if you live in the centre of London or New York. . . . I happen to live in the middle of rural Dorset.

If you do have a dry cleaner conveniently nearby make sure he specialises in individual treatment. Ask to see the 'special attention' director and show him your piece. If you feel hesitant, ask him to try a piece of extra of the same fabric first.

Q: Can I press my work?
A: Yes, you certainly can – but remember that 'caution always pays'.

I have already mentioned the time I stupidly scorched a panel into which I had poured hours and hours' stitching time. . . .

I personally prefer a steam iron, but if you like working with a dry iron I suggest you use a dry pressing cloth. Place it between the iron and the item to help prevent scorching.

When I am dealing with something worked with stranded cottons on Glenshee, I press on the front of the fabric. I 'nose' the iron right up to the stitched motifs but I try to avoid actually putting pressure ON those motifs and not flatten the stitching.

And every time you start pressing, I suggest you 'try' the heat of the iron either on a waste scrap of similar fabric, or on a corner or seam of the actual cloth.

Q: Do I have to 'block' my work?
A: 'Blocking', pulling back into shape, should not be necessary with linen

items. Since the fabric should not distort during working the shape should be more or less the same as when you started stitching.

If an old sampler or cloth has been nailed in a frame for many years then distortion – pulling points around the edges of the item towards those nails – might have occurred, and it is practically impossible to remove.

Q: What is the best way of displaying my finished piece.
A: Be traditional. If you are working a sampler, for instance, nothing looks nicer than a sampler behind a traditional *frame*. The choice of framing can make or mar the effect of the whole piece.

I prefer a card mount, a 'window frame' separating the sampler from the main frame. If you have a good framing shop near you I suggest you take your piece along and ask advice on complementary mounting and framing colours/types. Make sure that you tell the expert about the colour scheme of the room in which you want your piece to hang.

After you have spent hours, if not days, weeks or even longer, stitching a piece, it may be necessary to have a 'fresh eye' to choose suitable mounting and framing. I finished a sampler as a house-guest-present when staying with dear friends outside Buffalo, New York. It was the Buffalo framer who suggested a mount that matched one small motif in my design and a rustic wooden frame to symbolise the garden indicated in the sampler's design. I would have chosen something far more usual – and far less effective.

Q: If I have no frame to hand, can I do it myself?
A: Of course you can. If you have a handyman in the house you can call on him for help in making a frame. If not, go to a chain store and purchase a photograph frame several sizes bigger than your finished piece. Go to an art shop and get a piece of mounting board in a suitable colour.

To Do the Framing Yourself You Will Need:

finished piece

frame

mounting board

piece of dark paper

masking tape

sharp knife or scissors

ruler

1 Take the 'paper filler' out of the photograph frame and, using this as a pattern, cut an area of mounting board.

2 Measure the stitched area of your piece – say 30 × 10 cm (12 × 4 in). Cut a window in the prepared mount, as centrally as possible, 3 cm (just

over 1 in) taller and 2 cm (just under 1 in) wider than the stitched area –
say 33 × 12 cm (13¼ × 5 in).

3 Put the mounting board in the frame, right side to the glass.

4 The easiest way of correctly placing the sampler is then to lay it, right
side to the glass, so that there is more 'surplus' fabric showing at the top
than at the bottom. There should be equal amounts of surplus showing
either side of the stitched area.

5 Hold the sampler in place with strips of masking tape, stuck to the
surplus on the back of the sampler and extending to the back of the
mounting board.

6 Since dark embroidery thread 'ends' may show through your linen, cut
a dark paper shape, using the frame's paper 'filler' as pattern. Place this
dark paper behind the fabric.

7 Put the frame's own backing in place and seal as instructed.

Q: Have you any further mounting tips?
A: You would not believe – well, perhaps you would – how easy it is to
finish mounting a small picture. You seal the back of the frame securely
closed with mounting tape so that no air will get in for centuries to come,
you hang your treasure on the wall and, oh dear, you put the piece in the
frame upside down. . . .

Moral to that story is DO make sure you place your design right way up!

Similarly, if you are putting a favourite piece of cross stitching on a
chair seat, make sure the design faces you as you look at the chair from the
front.

Q: What are self-stick mounting boards?
A: In case some of you have not yet come across them, special art
needlework mounting boards are advertised in many magazines. Sheets
of what is rather like two-sided sticky tape already have one side stuck to a
strong board. Peel off the protective paper on the other side and you have
a sticky surface to which to adhere your cross stitch piece.

Boards come either with foam backing or plain and they can be cut to fit
any size piece.

Q: How do you feel about framing behind glass?
A: Traditionally samplers, for instance, *have* been framed behind glass
and cross stitch is one technique which does not suffer when so displayed.
(Such three-dimensional forms as raised or stumpwork, for example,
seem 'flatter' and satin stitching, with its silky sheen, loses impact when
placed behind glass.)

Samplers have survived for years and years behind glass. Don't you want
your piece – sampler or whatever – similarly to last for a long long time?

People have differing opinions about non-reflecting glass. I personally
do not use it as I think it makes the stitchery behind it look like a paper
photograph.

Q: Yes, but how can I show off a larger item?
A: Unless you have an available wall of museum proportions you will probably not be able completely to show, say, a large table cloth. (If you CAN, I suggest you contact your local museum for display ideas.)

Actually I think nothing looks nicer than a table cloth on a table. Why not show it off, at least from time to time? You can always take it off at mealtimes.

Q: Have you any other display ideas?
A: I have already mentioned setting small panels into photograph album or scrapbook covers. You can buy suitable 'framing' file covers in most American needlework shops.

Other possible framing ideas include putting a small piece of cloth on, say, a coffee table, and then getting a piece of bevelled glass cut the same size as the table top so that the cloth is held flat beneath the glass.

Q: I have too much cross stitch to display it all. How can I store it?
A: The main thing is to remember that creases in linen can become semi-permanent. Therefore, wherever possible, I suggest you avoid folding items which are to be put away.

Lay them flat or roll them around a cardboard filler taken from the inside of a roll of paper towels. (Cover the card with tissue paper first as some card contains acids potentially harmful to fabrics.) If you must fold pieces refold them in different places from time to time.

Store in a closed compartment – a drawer, a chest or cardboard box (lined with tissue paper). Make sure all pieces are kept *dry* and not too near excessive heat.

If you are hanging garments, cover metal parts of the hangers with tissue paper or fabric scraps. If you hang them in clear plastic garment bags make sure you pierce the bags several times to allow air to circulate.

Q: I have an old linen cloth with a hole in it. What can I do?
A: I have already explained how you can disguise a cut (see p. 12). If you have a *hole* there are various things you can do:

1 If the piece is displayed in a wall-hanging frame, why not put an attractive backing behind it and leave the hole? This is certainly a recommended solution for historic pieces.

   A canvaswork panel probably worked in the late sixteenth century by Mary, Queen of Scots, and now at Hardwick hall, has several holes in it. The green backing behind shows *intentionally* through the holes.

2 An idea suitable for a new piece is to work an appropriate motif, say a flower in similar colours to the decoration already on the cloth, on a scrap of fabric. This scrap can be applied to cover the hole.

3 Again, if you have a modern piece, you could employ traditional patching techniques to patch the hole.

4 If you want to disguise a hole by stitching you could carefully darn the hole, with close weavings in alignment to each warp and weft thread.

> *Don't forget to* strip *(the thread, that is). Pull out one strand and then another and lay as many strands together to achieve smoother, untwisted stitching*

Regardless of which kind of mending you may decide to do, you should hold the fabric taut on an embroidery frame or hoop during reparation.

Q: I have inherited an old sampler. Some of the stitches are missing. Can I work them in?
A: Up to you. If you are sure you know what was originally there – or intended – then go ahead. But to be authentic you should not make your own choice on how to 'extend' or alter the design. Perhaps your great grandmother *intended* the stitched dog only to have three legs!

Q: You give all these hints on how to look after pieces of cross stitch. Do all your comments refer to old pieces as well as new?
A: If you are in doubt about any home reparation on an old piece the answer is simple . . . *don't*. Better be safe than sorry.

There are excellent conservation bodies but they are costly and many of the conservation experts have a full diary for some time ahead.

If you want to read further about professional conservation I recommend:

> Karen Finch and Greta Putnam, *Caring for Textiles*, Barrie & Jenkins, 1977
>
> Harold F. Mailand, *Considerations for the Care of Textiles and Costumes*, Indianapolis Museum of Art, 1978.

You might also find that Jean M. Glover's *Textiles: their Care and Protection in Museums* (Museums Association, 1973) has addresses of suppliers which might be helpful to you.

Q: How can I find out how much that inherited piece of cross stitch work is worth?
A: It is easiest to get some indication of the worth of a piece if it is a sampler. Check relevant Sotheby Parke Bernet's and Christie's catalogues of the past few months and see what various items fetched.

If you are concerned with the possible current value of, say, a beautiful old table cloth or a cross-stitched blouse from Bosnia, you will possibly have to check through many more of the textiles catalogues from those auction houses.

Do not personally approach a sale room for an estimate unless you are seriously thinking of selling. The experts' time is precious and they are not there to give valuations to all and sundry. And I personally would not accept the valuation estimate of an antiques dealer – who might give *you* a bare minimum, buy the piece and then resell it for its real worth.

7 Beyond cross stitch

This chapter is a miscellany of ideas and creative suggestions. I offer several; if you think of other ways of expanding the number of different forms of cross stitch I should love to hear from you.

As well as such variants as crossed-corners cross stitch and other forms illustrated and described in Chapter 1, there are of course *standard variants on cross stitch*.

In this category I should include *velvet stitch*. This is one of the most lush members of the cross stitch family as it produces a looped pile which can either be left in loops or trimmed. There are several ways of doing it but I find my method the easiest and the most lasting (you do not want the cut stitches later to come away from your fabric). You need a pencil or similar tube and each loop is, as the diagrams show, worked around this to produce loops of even length.

Velvet stitch, formed around a pencil

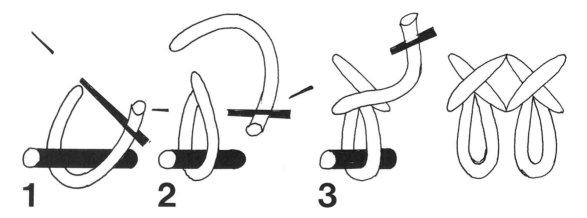

I find that velvet stitch is most effective when worked in conjunction with ordinary cross stitch. See, for instance, the photograph of the Wesley family tree picture. If you are, however, working a whole block of velvet stitch work the lowest line of stitching first. When you have worked this, form another line directly above so that the loops of this line cover the holding cross stitches of the previous row.

One of the greatest experimenters – indeed one of the most important needleworkers of all time – was Louisa Pesel (1870–1942), at one time

Right
A page of notes made by Louisa Pesel.
(*The Brotherton Library, University of Leeds*)

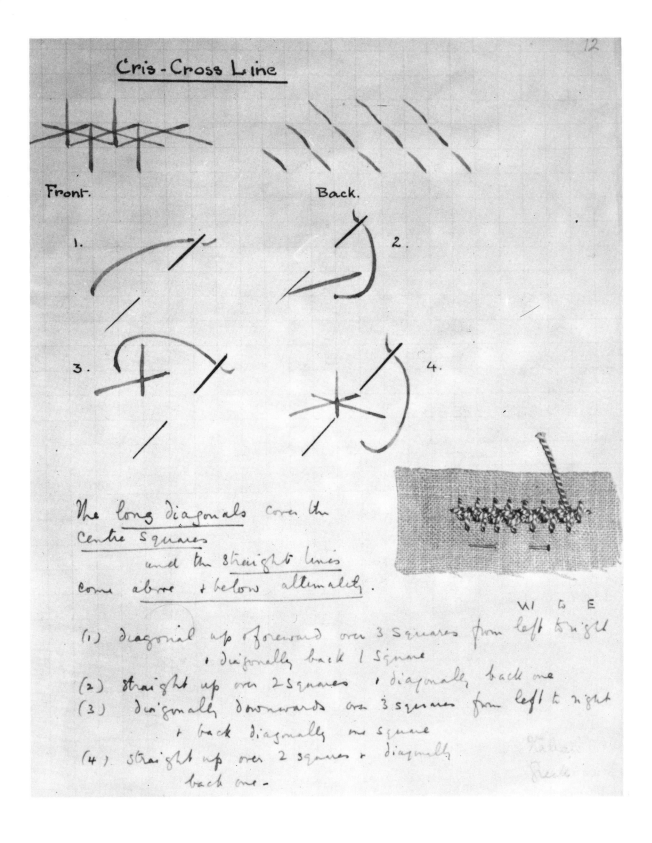

Cris-Cross Line

Front.   Back.

1.   2.

3.   4.

The long diagonals cover the
centre squares
          and the straight lines
come above + below alternately.

(1) diagonal up + forward over 3 squares from left to right
          + diagonally back 1 square
(2) straight up over 2 squares + diagonally back one.
(3) diagonally downwards over 3 squares from left to right
          + back diagonally one square
(4) straight up over 2 squares + diagonally
          back one.

Director of the Royal Hellenic Schools of Needlework and Lace in Athens. Her latest studies of traditional English stitches were commissioned by the Victoria & Albert Museum, where they can still be seen.

I had the good fortune a couple of years ago to be allowed to look through and study some of Miss Pesel's private notebooks and samples (stored in the Brotherton Library, University of Leeds). As the illustration of one of the pages of her notebooks shows, Miss Pesel carefully documented and worked up test pieces of stitches she had identified from various parts of the world. She annotated her own drawings and workings: 'criss-cross line stitch', she wrote, could be 'found on Italian and Greek needleworks'. (I have personally tried it and it produces a good, solid 'filling line'.)

Trying Miss Pesel's stitch encouraged me to see what *I* could do to vary ordinary cross stitch.

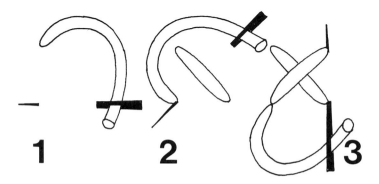
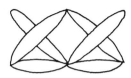

Underlined cross stitch

As my Olivetti ET221 typewriter has its own *underlining* capacity, I produced an *underlined* cross stitch. From this it is a simple step to producing cross stitches *in boxes*.

So I experimented with different stitch variations. I also tried working *cross stitch on different materials.* I designed a white organdie and satin lingerie pouch as a wedding present for Anne Littlejohn. (You can see it illustrated opposite p. 48.) I wanted to embellish the front of the pouch with a cross-stitched floral bouquet. How to work cross stitch on finely-woven organdie? That was the question. . . .

The solution was to use a 'vanishing pen'. This is a fibre pen which has a blue 'ink' that washes away to invisibility when cold water is applied.

To Make the Lingerie Pouch You Will Need:

32 × 95 cm ($12\frac{1}{2}$ × $37\frac{1}{2}$ in)

ie 31 × 24 cm (12 × $9\frac{1}{2}$ in)

Vanishing pen (In Britain, look for the Pikaby water-erasable marking pen)

Frame or hoop (I used my round, 10 cm, 4 in, diameter hoop)

1.5 m (5 ft) white satin ribbon 1 cm (nearly $\frac{1}{2}$ in) wide

All-purpose sewing thread (white)

1 skein each DMC 894 (darker pink), 963 (paler pink), 211 (pale purple), 209 (darker purple), 906 (green), 336 (dark blue), 799 (pale blue), 444 (yellow)

Pointed needle (I used Crewel 8).

First pin the organdie to a sheet of graph paper with 20 squares per 5 centimetre (10 per inch). Carefully make vanishing pen 'dots' at each junction of the graph paper. Remove the organdie.

How to stitch on organdie! Lay the fabric over graph paper and make dots above junctions of the paper's squares (1). Each cross stitch is later formed between four of your dots (2)

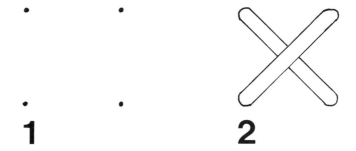

The blue ink will disappear when *cold water* is applied. This means that it is essential that you do *not* get the organdie wet while you are still stitching (so do not cry over it!).

Follow the chart in the usual way to work your cross stitch bouquet. You will probably find it easiest to place the part of the organdie on which you are currently working on the frame or hoop to hold it taut. *Two strands* – cross stitches worked *between four dots*. You are *not* counting organdie threads.

Take care that you do not take surplus thread from one part of the design to another. All starting and finishing of threads must be hidden in the back of worked areas. Any surplus threads will show when the near-transparent organdie is later placed above white satin.

In the space where I have stitched 'Rickie and Anne' you can similarly design and stitch your favoured inscription; you will find suitable alphabets on pp. 86–8.

When you have finished all the cross stitching, carefully place the organdie in *cold water* and the blue dots will disappear. Let the organdie dry – and carefully press it.

Lay the organdie on one end of the right side of the satin as illustrated. Tack the two fabrics together. Take a 2.5 cm (1 in) fold at the left of the organdie and machine stitch from top to bottom of the fabric.

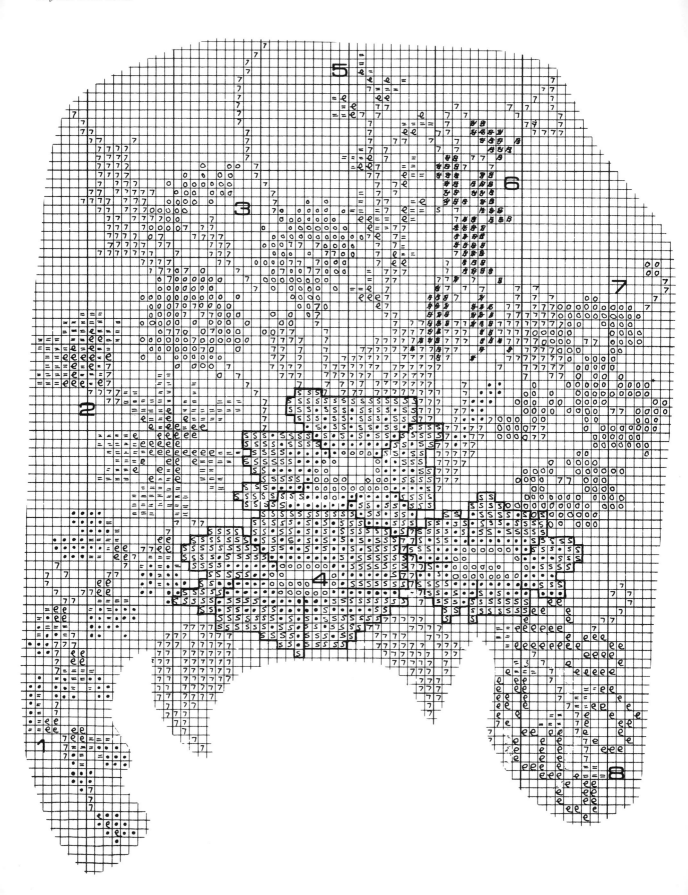

Fold the fabrics in half, bringing the sides of the shape together, organdie facing in. Make a sandwich by the usual method.

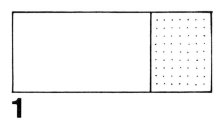

1

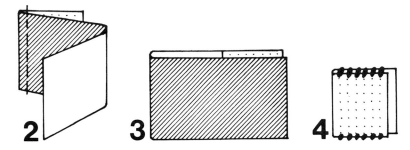

2   **3**   **4**

To make up the pouch, organdie (dotted) is laid on the satin, right sides up (1). The fabrics are folded, and machine stitched (back of fabrics shown shaded, 2). The fabrics are folded (3) and a sandwich formed. The piece is subsequently held with overstitching (4)

Fold the sandwich vertically at the left of the organdie. You should have about a 2 cm ($\frac{7}{8}$ in) extension at the lower flap. Overstitch the top and bottom of the front to the back of the pouch and attach lengths of ribbon to form side ties and bows.

✩✩✩✩✩✩✩✩✩

Other ideas relating to this project:

1 You could work the same floral bouquet in silver and white as a silver wedding present.

2 Instead of making a lingerie pouch, you could make the finished stitching up into a small cushion or a cover for a photograph album.

✩✩✩✩✩✩✩✩✩

Left
The floral bouquet features (1) wild pea, *Lathyrus sylvestris* (2) common mallow, *Malva sylvestris* (3) dandelion, *Taraxacum officinale* (4) dog rose, *Rosa canina* (5) common calamint, *Calamintha ascendens* (6) bluebell, *Endymion non-scriptus* (7) common meadow buttercup, *Ranunculus acris* and (8) wood vetch *Vicia sylvatica*:

7	green	e	darker purple
●	bright pink	s	pale pink
×	dark blue	#	pale blue
=	pale purple	○	yellow

– all outlining back stitches in dark blue

I also tried another method of stitching on non-evenweave. Do you remember the 'waste canvas' to which I referred in Chapter 2? Well, today it is an easy matter to *produce your own waste canvas* if, that is, you cannot buy any locally.

I took an area of single-weave canvas with 44 threads per 5 centimetres (22 threads per inch) and *washed it to remove sizing*. Try washing a small sample and you can see how easy it is to remove warp and weft threads one by one.

How to stitch with waste canvas. The canvas is laid above fabric and stitches worked through both materials (1), after which canvas threads are withdrawn one by one (2)

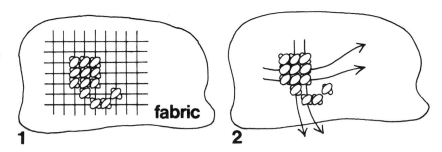

fabric

1   **2**

I stitched the rose on my calico hostess apron by stitching over waste canvas tacked to the calico. When I had finished all cross stitching I carefully pulled out each of the canvas threads.

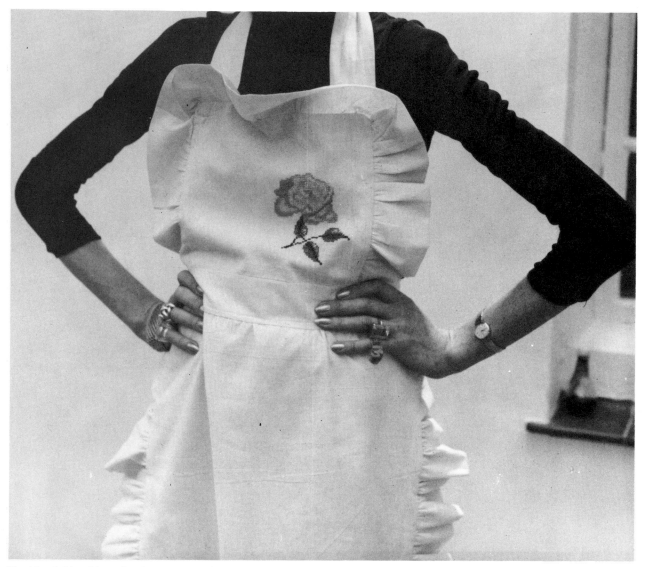

The bib of this white calico hostess apron has a Peace rose worked over 'waste canvas'

This project combines two experiments. I was impatient with the generally-accepted constraint of working both diagonals of a stitch in the same colour thread so I experimented with *working diagonals of a stitch in different colours*. As you will see from the complicated graph, one stitch might have a yellow lower diagonal and an orange upper diagonal. Just think how many delicate shading permutations are therefore possible. . . .

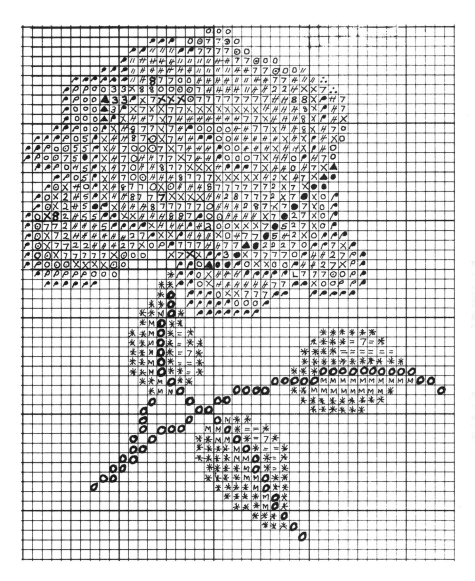

The Peace rose on my apron bib was worked with cross stitches of mostly differently-coloured diagonals:

blue uppers
●   blue over blue
3   blue over orange

pink uppers
ℙ   pink over pink
p   pink over orange
∴   pink over cream

orange uppers
○   orange over orange
▲   orange over blue
ς   orange over pink
⊙   orange over yellow

yellow uppers
7   yellow over yellow
L   yellow over pink
×   yellow over orange
2   yellow over cream

cream uppers
//   cream over cream
5   cream over blue
//   cream over orange
8   cream over yellow

dark green uppers
O   dark green over dark green

bright green uppers
*   bright green over bright green
M   bright green over dark green
=   bright green over yellow

To Make the Calico Apron and Headscarf You Will Need:

2.30 m (2½ yd) unbleached calico 96 cm (38 in) wide

3 cm (1¼ in) matching touch-and-close fastening

All-purpose sewing thread (off-white).

First prepare appropriate shapes of calico as indicated. Tack washed 'waste canvas' to one bib front. Follow the complicated graph to stitch the rose (*2 strands* over *2 canvas threads*, stitching through calico too). Remove tackings, and canvas threads.

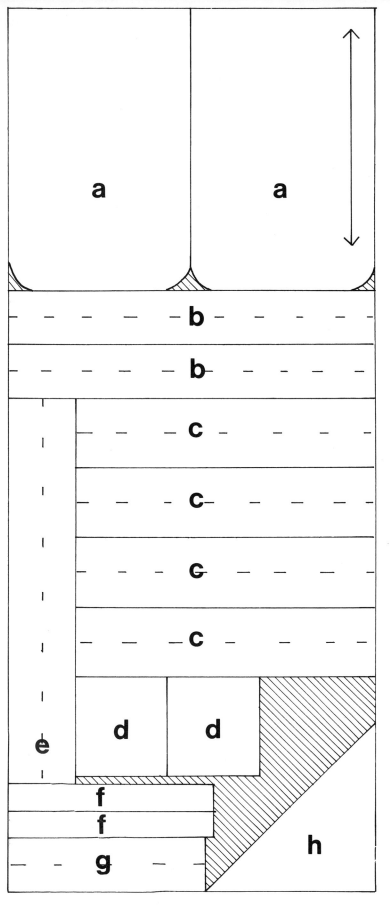

Cutting diagram for the apron and headscarf. *2.54 cm = 20 cm fabric* (1 in = 8 in fabric):

a skirt
b waist ties (later to be folded on dogted lines)
c skirt ruffs
d bibs
e bib ruff
f waist fronts
g neck band
h headscarf

Right
To make up the apron (wrong side of fabric shaded)

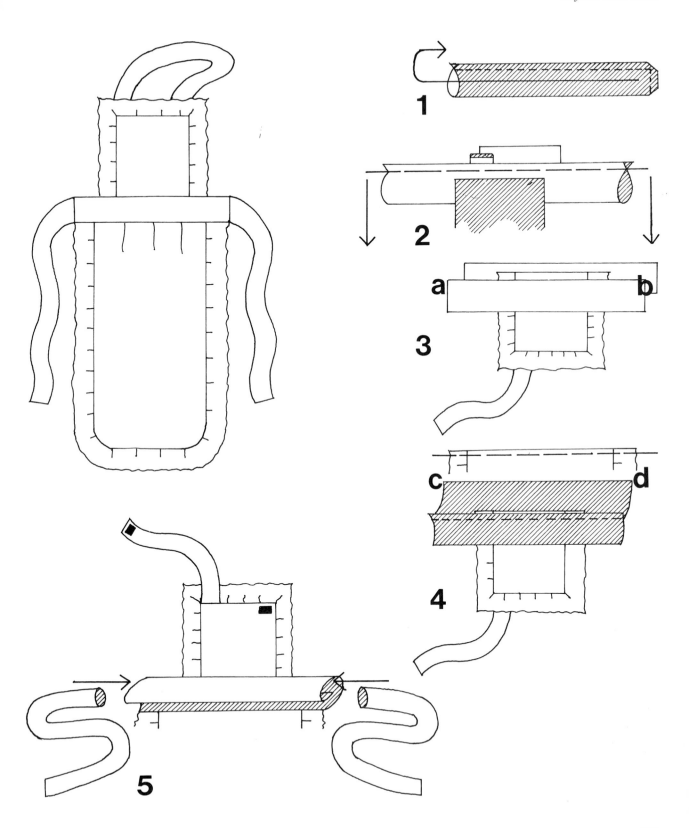

1

2

a   b

3

c   d

4

5

Make tubes, with one end sealed, of the neckband and both waist tie shapes. Snip corners and turn the shapes right sides out (diagram 1).

Gather the bib ruff, right side out, and make a sandwich of both bib shapes, wrong sides out, with a filling of the ruff and the open end of the neckband strip as indicated (diagram 2). Stitch along both vertical sides and along the upper horizontal side of the sandwich and turn it right side out. Make a similar sandwich of the two skirt shapes, wrong sides out, and a filling of a long ruff formed of the four skirt ruff shapes joined together. Turn the skirt area right side out.

Make another sandwich of the two waist front shapes, wrong sides out, and the open end of the prepared bib area (diagram 3). Stitch AB.

Join the long side of one of the waist fronts to the gathered open end of the prepared skirt area (diagram 4) and stitch CD.

Bring the other waist front shape down to the CD stitch line. Turn under a surplus 1 cm (nearly $\frac{1}{2}$ in) and hem. Insert the open ends of the waist ties in the ends of the waist front tube, surplus 1 cm (nearly $\frac{1}{2}$ in) turned in, and similarly hem. Place one of the touch-and-close fastening strips on the reverse side of the unattached end of the neckband and the other strip on the reverse side of the top of the main bib shape as indicated (diagram 5).

To assemble the headscarf, machine or hand-hem along all three sides to prevent fraying.

☆☆☆☆☆☆☆☆☆☆

I had not worked any cross stitches on ordinary *canvas* for some time, so I thought up a little blackwork motif adapted from a brass rubbing, 42.7 cm (17 in) high, as a memorial to Margaret Peyton, who died in 1484. Her memorial can be seen in the church at Isleham, Cambridge.

To Work a Blackwork On Canvas Motif You Will Need:

Area single canvas 20 cm (8 in) square, 44 threads per 5 centimetres (22 per in) – I used British yellow canvas

Hard lead pencil

2 skeins DMC 3371 (black)

Tapestry 24 needle.

First lay the canvas above the motif and trace outlines through. Follow the *line* as you trace; do not necessarily 'count threads'.

Cross stitch all sections of the design as indicated, *1 or 2 strands* over *2 canvas threads*. Then stitch all traced outlines in chain stitch, *2 strands*.

☆☆☆☆☆☆☆☆☆☆

My Margaret Peyton piece combines cross stitch with chain stitch. This

> *Always leave a needle* threaded. *Then it is easier to find it when it is lost*

Margaret Peyton (died 1484) – a stitched picture from a brass rubbing. Picture 15×13 cm (6×5 in)

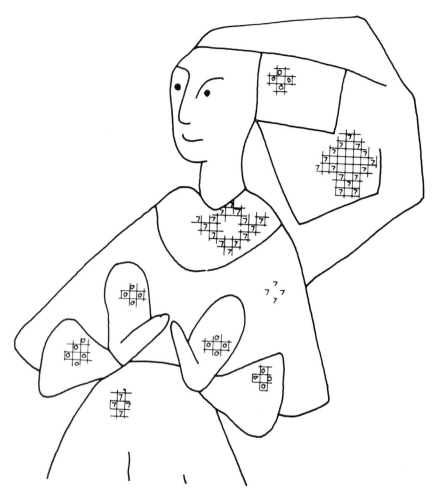

Lady Margaret Peyton. As you can see from the accompanying photograph, cross stitches were worked with one or two strands:

7   1 strand
○   2 strands

marriage encouraged me to *combine cross with other stitch forms*. The result is the quintessential sampler with which I end this chapter. You can see it illustrated as a colour photograph.

I drew the same oak leaf shape five times. In one I worked a *blackwork* cross stitch design. In another, I worked *trapunto* by stitching an area of white lawn to the back of the motif. I worked running stitches through both layers, outlining the leaf and its main vein. I covered these running stitches with cross stitches, and padded the two leaf sections by making slits in the lawn and putting in paddings from the rear.

A third leaf I worked in *shadow whitework*. I worked small running stitches all around the leaf's shape. I cut the leaf out, leaving a 1 cm (nearly ½ in) surplus, in which I cut small V snips as necessary to accommodate curves, and turned the surplus under. Then I tacked an area of organdie behind the hole. I worked tiny cross stitches all round the leaf's shape, thus holding the organdie permanently to the linen. I drew in veins with a vanishing pen, worked them in cross stitch, and moistened the area to remove the blue vanishing pen marks.

A fourth leaf combines cross stitch with *appliqué*. I cut out a felt leaf shape and applied it with cross stitches. The last leaf introduces *metal thread, couching and beadwork*. I laid my metal thread around the leaf's shape and held it in place with tiny cross couching stitches. Beads are dotted in one of the leaf's sections.

✩✩✩✩✩✩✩✩✩✩

The versatility of cross stitch is never-ending. Happy stitching!

Suggested further reading

You will have seen that some specialist books are included in the relevant part of the text; they are all entered in the index at the back of the book under the name of the author.

General books in cross stitch that you might enjoy are:

Gerda Bengtsson, *Herbs and Medicinal Plants in Cross-Stitch from the Danish Handcraft Guild*. Van Nostrand Reinhold, 1979
Counted Cross Stitch Patterns and Designs, Bell & Hyman, 1981

Irmgard Gierl, *Cross Stitch Patterns*, Batsford, 1977

Thelma Nye, *Cross Stitch Patterns*, Batsford, 1969

Hildy Paige Burns and Kathleen Thorne-Thomsen, *American Cross-Stitch*, Van Nostrand Reinhold, 1974.

The main *exclusively counted thread* publication is *Counted Thread*, quarterly publication of The Counted Thread Society, 3305 South Newport Street, Denver Co 80224 USA.

Among relevant foreign magazines for which you might like to look out are the Danish *Symed Korssting* and the Dutch *Ariadne Kruissteken* (ask Kay Montclare or Bette Feinstein – see addresses overleaf).

Mail order suppliers

The *Danish Handcraft Guild*'s address is:

Danish Handcraft Guild
38 Wimmelskaftet
1161 Copenhagen K
Denmark.
(You can buy their Danish flower thread from the mail order suppliers below.)

The following sell most of the cross stitch materials mentioned in this book (all have catalogues and offer mail order facilities):

U.K.

The Danish House
16 Sloane Street
London SW1X 9NB

The Silver Thimble
33 Gay Street
Bath, Avon BA1 2NT

USA

The Counting House
Box 155
Pawleys Island SC 29585

Kay Montclare
World in Stitches
82 South Street
Milford, NH 03055

Frederick Fawcett Inc.
129 South Street, Boston Ma. 0211

New and old foreign books and magazines can be obtained from:

Bette Feinstein
96 Roundwood
Newton, MA 02164

☆☆☆☆☆☆☆☆☆

For full details of *Mary Gostelow's own sampler designs* please send a first class stamp to:

Sew-a-Sampler
43 Milton Abbas
Blandford Dorset England.

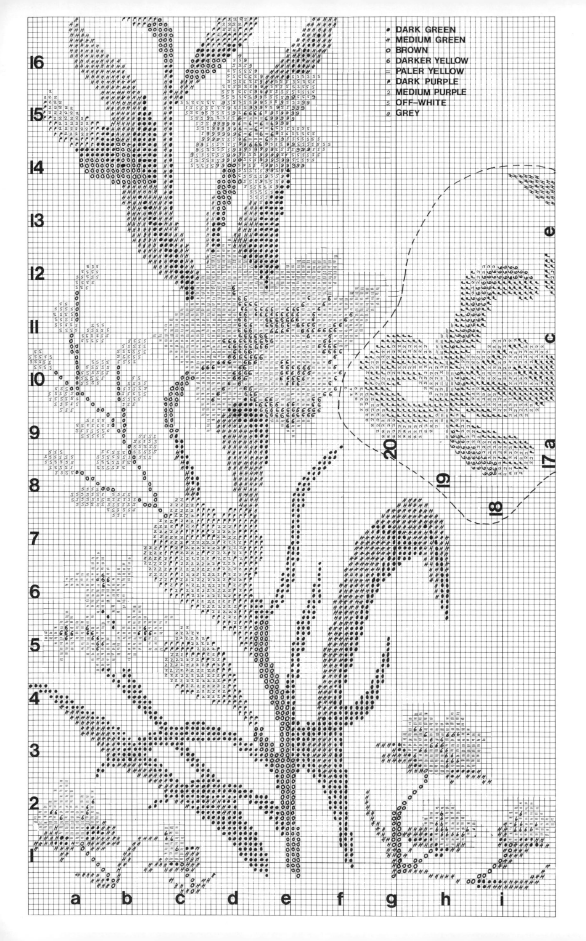

DARK GREEN
MEDIUM GREEN
BROWN
DARKER YELLOW
PALER YELLOW
DARK PURPLE
MEDIUM PURPLE
OFF-WHITE
GREY

Index